XB/CO/IP

45-

D1600364

THE
CAVALIER
ARMY

1. Sir George Wharton, Royalist and astrologer, defeated at Stow-on-the-Wold in 1643 (*City Art Gallery, York, the collection of the late Lord Wharton*)

THE
CAVALIER
ARMY

Its Organisation
and Everyday Life

by
BRIGADIER PETER YOUNG
DSO, MC, MA, FSA

and

WILFRID EMBERTON
FRGS, AR Hist. S

With twenty-four line illustrations
by Stephen Beck

London
GEORGE ALLEN & UNWIN LTD
Ruskin House   Museum Street

ISBN 0 04 942124 7

Printed in Great Britain
in 11 point Baskerville
by W & J Mackay Limited
Chatham

To the memory of
JOHN M. EMBERTON DCM
*who in his generation braved worse
hazards than the men whose adventures
are described here*

Foreword

'God must have loved the Common Man –
He made so many of them'

Abraham Lincoln

In this book we have striven to show what it was like to serve in the army of King Charles I. It has not been altogether an easy task. For this there are two main reasons. The first is prejudice: the second is information – or rather lack of it.

As to prejudice we will only say that the familiar and conventional idea of a Cavalier or of a Roundhead is a gross caricature. There were, of course, rakehells on the one side and ranting hypocrites on the other, but for the most part the men who were drawn into the struggle were in their day typical of their region, their class, or their family. In the so-called permissive society of today the great majority on either side would probably be regarded as extremely strait-laced.

As to information it may be worth remarking that for any war after the Napoleonic Wars one can usually find numbers of eyewitness accounts, letters, diaries and so on, to illustrate the smallest action. This is not so of the Civil War. One cannot, for example, find so much as a single letter describing the battle of Naseby from the point of view of a Royalist infantry officer. In building up our picture we have been compelled to range far and wide in the search to present a comprehensive picture of the seventeenth-century service-man's life, his pleasures, punishments and privations from the time of joining to his pension.

Whilst sometimes we have been compelled to tread relatively familiar ground, we hope we have opened up new vistas in some directions. The combinations of our very different service backgrounds and attitudes has perhaps resulted in a real contribution not only to Civil War literature, but to the growing interest in social history as well. In a work of this nature one is greatly assisted by the help freely and generously given by all kinds of people too numerous to name here, but we feel that the significant contribution made by two ladies cannot be overlooked. Our grateful thanks to Joan Young, who read and corrected the proof copy, and Janet Walker, who grappled with the handwriting of which-ever one of us it was.

P.Y.
W.J.E.

Contents

Illustrations

1642

3 January	King Charles enters Parliament to arrest the Five Members
23 April	Hull closes her gates against the King
21 August	Dover Castle taken by Parliament forces
22 August	The King raises his standard at Nottingham
7 September	Waller takes Portsmouth from Goring
23 September	Skirmish at Powick Bridge. Rupert routs Parliamentary horse
23 October	First major confrontation, at Edgehill. Royalist victory
29 October	Oxford becomes Royalist headquarters
12 November	Rupert storms and takes Brentford
13 November	King's army confronted by conjoined forces of Essex and the London Trained Bands. King retreats to Reading
12 December	Waller captures Winchester

1643

19 January	Braddock Down. Hopton secures Cornwall for the King
2 February	Rupert storms Cirencester
23 February	The Queen lands at Bridlington
19 March	Northampton defeats Gell and Brereton at Hopton Heath, but is slain
13 April	Maurice defeats Waller at Ripple
21 April	Rupert takes Lichfield
25 April	Reading falls to Essex
25 April	Chudleigh defeats Hopton at Sourton Down
16 May	Hopton defeats Stamford at Stratton
21 May	Fairfax surprises Goring at storming of Wakefield
18 June	Chalgrove Field. Hampden mortally wounded
29 June	Newcastle routs the Fairfaxes at Adwalton Moor
5 July	Hopton defeats Waller at Lansdown
13 July	Wilmot and Maurice rout Waller at Roundway Down
26 July	Nathaniel Fiennes surrenders Bristol to Rupert

10 August to 5 September	The King besieges Gloucester which is relieved by Essex
20 September	The King's attempt to block Essex's route to London foiled in marginal Parliament victory at First Newbury
25 September	Parliament enlists Scottish aid by signing the Solemn League and Covenant
11 October	Widdrington and Henderson defeated by Manchester, Sir Thomas Fairfax and Cromwell at Winceby
9 December	Arundel Castle taken by Hopton

1644

6 January	Arundel Castle retaken by Waller
19 January	Scots enter England as allies of Parliament
25 January	Sir Thomas Fairfax relieves the siege of Nantwich by defeating Byron
21 March	Relief of Newark. Rupert captures Meldrum
29 March	Waller decisively defeats Forth and Hopton in a major confrontation at Cheriton
11 April	Belasyse defeated by Sir Thomas Fairfax at Selby
29 June	Cropredy Bridge. Waller defeated by the King
2 July	Rupert and Newcastle overwhelmingly defeated at Marston Moor by the combined forces of Leven (Scots), Fairfax and Manchester in biggest battle of war. Cromwell virtual architect of victory. North lost to the King
16 July	Glemham surrenders York to Fairfax
21 August	The King defeats Essex at Lostwithiel
21 August	The King again defeats Essex at Fowey
2 September	Essex escapes by sea, leaving Skippon to surrender army
27 October	The King, heavily outnumbered by Manchester, Waller and Cromwell, holds them off and retreats by night at Second Newbury
6 November	Rupert commissioned Lieutenant-General of all the Royalist armies
9 November	Donnington Castle relieved by Rupert
19 December	Self-Denying Ordinance passed by Parliament

1645

19 February	Maurice relieves Chester

22 February	Parliament forces under Mytton take Shrewsbury
Early April	New Model Army formed from the forces of Manchester, Essex and Waller, who resign
30 May	Royalists storm Leicester
14 June	The Royalist cause virtually lost at Naseby. King's army totally defeated and dispersed by New Model Army under Sir Thomas Fairfax
17 June	Leicester taken by Fairfax
10 July	Fairfax defeats Goring at Langport
10 September	Rupert surrenders Bristol to Fairfax
24 September	Defeat of Royalists at Rowton Heath
14 October	Cromwell storms Basing House

1646

13 March	Hopton surrenders to Fairfax at Falmouth
21 March	Astley surrenders last Royalist army at Stow-on-the-Wold
5 May	King surrenders to the Scots at Southwell
25 June	Surrender of Oxford

Chapter One

Raising the Army

Recruit me Lancashire and Cheshire both,
And Derbyshire hills that are so free . . .

King Henry V in 'The Ballad of Agincourt'

England in August 1642 was in the midst of harvest, the fields covered in shocks of corn or standing golden brown ready for the sickle. But the time had come for another and bitter harvest. The long months of move and counter move between King Charles and his Parliament were over, culminating with the monarch's leading armed men into the House of Commons to arrest five members, his chief opponents, only to find his birds flown. Now, with the raising of the royal standard at Nottingham on 22 August, the country lay under the shadow of fratricidal Civil War.

Both sides had covertly started recruiting earlier in the year, when it had become increasingly obvious that their differences could only be settled by force of arms. The country had been at peace for over seventy years and, as Lord Cecil had remarked, the knowledge and almost the thought of war was extinguished. However, the military virtues and experience of the English had not altogether lacked employment, for there were always the continental wars and those that followed the profession of arms saw service under the flags of Sweden, Holland, Denmark, Austria and even Russia. It was these returning warriors who stiffened and trained the fledgling armies of King and Parliament, their invaluable experience securing them swift promotion. The Parliament, busy raising its forces under the cloak of subduing Ireland, sought further to justify its activities by drawing public attention to the Royalist recruiting. On 20 May it made this declaration:

'It appears that the King seduced by wicked council intends to make war against his Parliament; and in pursuance thereof under pretence of a guard for his person has actually begun to levy forces both of horse and foot and sent out summonses throughout Yorkshire and other counties for calling out great numbers; and some ill affected persons have been employed in other parts to raise troops under colour of the King's service.'[1]

Charles had, in fact, used the genuine legal tactic of raising levies by use of the medieval process of issuing Commissions of Array to influential persons in every county upon whose support he felt he could rely. These Commissions called upon them to hold musters, view arms and to report their findings to the King. It was useful to him as a gauge of loyalty, but it was, however phrased, nothing less than a general call to arms.

Now came a testing time for all men of authority, from the great lords to the Justices of the Peace and country squires, for the Parliament had issued a statement saying that as the King seemed bent on making war on them, therefore they must act to preserve the peace and the King's subjects were instructed that, in Charles's own interest, they must accept no order that did not come from Parliament. 'Now there is so much declared as makes all officers in the Kingdom traitors to one side or another,' observed Sir Thomas Knyvett. The classic view, which goes back at least to the days of S. R. Gardiner, is that the King found his support in the north and west while backing for the Parliamentarian cause came from London, the Home Counties and East Anglia. Researches over the last thirty years have not radically altered this view, but like all generalities it is not entirely true. There were Cavaliers even in the strongest Roundhead areas. In Bedfordshire, for example, there were the Earl of Cleveland, a Royalist brigadier, and his son Lord Wentworth, major-general of the horse, as well as Sir Lewis Dyve, a colonel of foot; while from Hertfordshire came Lord Capel, from Essex the Lucas family and from Suffolk Colonel Thomas Blagge. The same was true of the Royalist districts. Then, as now, a political party tended to have a nucleus everywhere, but on the whole regional support for one side or the other was more clear-cut than it would be nowadays. As much of the Royalist support was traditionalist and conservative, it follows that the King's men came from the less populous and less developed parts of the country. Accustomed as we are to the amenities of the twentieth century, with its smooth tarmac roads, large population and mass media, it would be as well to reflect that in seventeenth-century England roads were rutted and muddy, the population was small, there were no newspapers as we know them, and few people who could have read them if they had been available, while the Post existed only in a rudimentary fashion.

There is really no reliable guide to the population of England and Wales earlier than the Hearth Tax Rolls of William III's reign. At that time it was about 5 million. In 1642 these islands probably held no more than 4½ million, but despite fluctuations due, for example, to the plague, the distribution probably did not differ greatly between the days of Charles I and William III. London, with something like half a million people, was overwhelmingly the largest and most important city. Bristol, the second city, had scarcely 30,000, while Norwich numbered not more than 14,000.

The war attracted a large number of foreign supporters, most of whom had come over not because they cared particularly about the islanders' squabbles, but because they were attracted by the prospect of booty. The Cavaliers seem to have recruited their quota of these, for Colonel Walter Slingsby describes the Queen's regiment of horse as being 'most French'. While obviously there must have been some Englishmen who fought in the hope of making their fortune, for the literate classes at least, conscience was the usual guide. Evidence for this may be gained by an examination of the records of most of the families who engaged in the fighting.

The eldest son of Sir Edmund Verney, the Knight Marshal who died bearing the Banner Royal at Edgehill, was for Parliament, while both younger sons were Royalists. The Cavalier Earl of Denbigh, killed at Birmingham, was succeeded by a Roundhead son. All the elder branch of the Cromwell family were for the King and at least six bore arms for him. Divided families are evidence of the strong feeling aroused by the struggle and the willingness to fight for the principles involved even against the judgement of parents and brothers. Happy the family that was united behind one party or the other, such as the Comptons and Byrons on the King's side and the Fairfaxes and Fiennes on Parliament's side. For most it was a difficult decision, typified by a Roundhead soldier who wrote, 'When I put my hand to the Lord's work, I did not do it rashly, but had many an hour and night to seek God to ask my way.' It was difficult for the educated upper strata of society who were bound to make a decision sooner or later by virtue of their official position, but it was a simpler task for the land-bound rustics who made up the bulk of the armies. Their thought, comfortably conditioned by landlord, vicar or pastor, and further shaped by the gossip of the local tavern where the news, exaggerated and distorted almost beyond belief, was given out by wayfarers, made it comparatively simple to come to a decision or even, in the initial stages of the conflict, to shelve it altogether.

The forces that influenced men's choice may be broadly classified under the following headings:

(a) *Politics*. Had the King been led astray by evil ministers and under their influence strayed so far from his duty that his judgement could no longer be trusted, leaving Parliament no alternative but to rule in his stead until he could be supplied with honest councillors? Or was Parliament a set of droning rascals who had only taken arms against the King to avoid a just retribution for their sins?

(b) *Religion*. Cromwell said: 'Religion was not a thing at first contested for, but God brought it to that issue at last; and gave it unto us by way of redundancy; and at last proved that which was most dear to us.' The religious issue was at least as strong as the political one. The Anglican family could be very largely relied on to be Royalist, while the Presbyterians and Independents were the backbone of the Parliamentary faction. Not a few turned to Parliament because they suspected the King of Roman Catholicism. True, his observation of the Protestant faith was immaculate, but the Queen was a confessed Catholic as were her followers. If the King permitted this in his own family, might he not be a secret Papist?

(c) *Divine right*. Akin to (b), but with a very special slant. There were those who held that the King ruled by divine appointment as Saul the first King of Israel had done. 'I beseech you to consider Majesty is sacred,' wrote young Edmund Verney to his elder brother. The opposing view was that Kings rule by the grace of God and the will of the people, that the Lord's Anointed and the man Charles Stuart were merged into one, and that when it came to law the latter was as liable to answer for his deeds as anyone.

(d) *Custom*. Being brought up as a tenant farmer or servant on a great estate would impose an obligation to serve as the landlord directed. Obviously the latter would leave a number of men to tend the fields and stock, or his ability to pay his regiment might be impaired; but few dependants would be spirited enough to deny military service to their lord on his chosen side.

Obviously many men fell between these categories, as has been remarked. There were the ambitious politicians, dissolute self-seeking courtiers, unemployed mercenaries and even bored younger sons spoiling for a fight. It could even be suggested that some found themselves involved merely by force of circumstance, who having perhaps listened to gossip that told a tale of local outrage joined in a hot-headed fit. Later in the war both sides used the equivalent of the press gang.

ORGANISATION

All over the country, Commissions of Array were being read by loyal men doing their duty, often in the most ill advised places. The Lord Mayor of London had his proclaimed in the city and was promptly stripped of his office and sent to the Tower, while Lord Chandos was driven out of Cirencester and his coach demolished. In Leicester the Mayor arrested the messenger and prevented him from making the proclamation, but on the credit side, the Yorkshire Fairfaxes were rebuffed by the King's officers and the Earl of Huntingdon's son successfully proclaimed the Commission in Leicester, but failed to raise the city as he had hoped. But although the Commissions of Array may have enabled the King and his staff to estimate where their support lay, the actual raising of the army was done by the issuing of commissions to raise regiments in a fashion that was modern rather than medieval.

The colonel, more often than not, decided whom he would appoint as his company officers and obtained the King's commissions for them. One such commission reads:

Charles, by the Grace of God, King of Great Britayne, Ffraince and Ireland, defender of the faith, etc. to our trustye and welbeloved Roger Whitley, Greeting. Wee doe hereby constitute and appoynt you to bee Captayne of one Troope of horse under the Regt. of our trusty and well beloved Colonell Charles Gerrard. The which troope by virtue of this commission you are forthwith to imprest and retayn such as will willingly and voluntarily serve us for our pay . . .

'Money,' as Charles was to remark, 'is the sinews of war'— and he had little enough of it. Queen Henrietta Maria, a woman of great spirit, went to Holland and pawned the Crown Jewels. With the proceeds she bought arms and the services of trained officers. The great nobles supplied the King with money. The Marquis of Newcastle is said to have spent a million pounds in the Royalist cause, while the Marquis of

Worcester, who owned most of Monmouthshire and lived in feudal splendour at Raglan Castle, advanced over a hundred thousand pounds by the end of the summer and was to advance eight times that amount by the end of the war. The 12-year-old Prince of Wales was sent on a fund-raising mission to Raglan and a good ambassador he proved to be, making merry with the local gentry, drinking the home brewed local liquor of fermented honey called metheglin and, with ineffable condescension, receiving their contributions to the war chest. The Oxford colleges contributed their plate, as did many a loyal heart in manor and hall. The University of Cambridge was about to follow suit when Cromwell stopped it forcibly. Thomas Bushell, 'Warden of our Mint and M[aste]r Worker of our Mynes Royall', undertook to coin silver at the rate of £1,000 weekly and to found cannon and cast shot in his foundries.

With the war chest reasonably full the next essential was men and arms. Forty peers guaranteed to pay a troop of horse for three months, although a few defaulted. The organisation of regiments was straightforward if a little cumbersome. In theory the regiments were very strong by modern standards, but after the first campaign only the most fortunate Royalist colonel could show 500 foot or 300 horse on his muster rolls.

The Horse

Ideally a regiment consisted of 500 volunteers, but was seldom at full strength, particularly in the later stages of the war. According to the popularity of the leader, the troops were of varying strength. Prince Rupert managed to keep his at full strength but this was a rarity and a tribute to his genius. Normally a regiment would consist of 6 troops each containing 70 officers and men, a total of 420. Of the officers three would be of field rank, that is to say, colonel, lieutenant-colonel and major. The latter dealt with all the regiment's paperwork, fulfilling the function later delegated to the adjutant, a post not to be created until the time of Charles II. These three officers were also troop commanders and the breakdown of a theoretical troop was:[2]

Troop commander (Field officer or captain)	1
Lieutenant	1
Cornet (carried the colour)	1
Quartermaster	1
Corporals	3
Trumpeters	2
Farriers	1
Troopers	60

The Foot

Ideally a regiment would consist of 10 companies, although in practice there might be 8 or fewer, each commanded as in the horse by a field officer or captain. The ordinary soldiers co-operated either as pikemen or musketeers, ideally in the ratio of 1 pikeman to every 2 musketeers. In the beginning, how-ever, it would seem that in many companies the numbers were about equal. One finds people with jobs peculiar to the times such as the gentleman-of-the-arms, whose function, as his name suggests, was the care of arms which were as scarce as gold at the beginning of the war. There were waggon masters, quartermasters, surgeons (chirurgeons) and chaplains whose tasks are self-evident. Towards the end the Royalist regiments dwindled in size and one even finds a company of

Give fire! King Charles's 'Life Guard of Foote' in action

colonels fighting together under the command of the senior colonel, as their own commands had been decimated.

The chain of command for a normal company was:

Captain (or field officer)[3]	1
Lieutenant	1
Ensign (who bore the colours)	1
Gentleman-of-the-arms	1
Sergeant	2
Corporals	3
Drummers	2

The companies were not equal in size. The colonel's company had 200 men, the lieutenant-colonel 160, the major 140 and each captain 100. Thus a full regiment would number 1,300 men.

The Dragoons

These were in fact mounted infantry, and were so called for the 'dragons', or short muskets, they carried. The horses they rode were generally of an inferior breed to the cavalry mount, for they were trained to fight on foot and were horsed only to lend them greater mobility. At Edgehill, the first battle of the Civil War, there were 3 regiments of dragoons. Their precise organisation is not certain, but the single dragoon regiment in the New Model Army had an establishment of 1,000 men organised in 10 companies.

Artillery

Cannon were most useful in siege work but counted little in battles. Their slow rate of fire, perhaps one round every three minutes if served by an expert crew, meant that there would have to be a great concentration to cause a decisive number of casualties. However, cannon did not exist in great numbers in the England of that time. At Edgehill the main Royalist force boasted only 20 and at Naseby, the last major battle, only 12. The equipment was heavy and expensive,[4] 'a sponge that can never be filled or satisfied', Clarendon called it. In transport the guns had no limber but were attached direct to a carriage consisting of an axle with two wheels and shafts as on a cart. Heavy draught horses or even oxen were harnessed in tandem and if the enclosed table is referred to, and related to the muddy, rutted state of the roads, it will not be surprising that their progress was slow. Primitive mortars were in existence, slow and dangerous to use but effective if all went well. The most popular gun for field use seems to have been the saker, weighing just over a ton and firing a relatively heavy shot. An attempt to make a more mobile gun was made by the Scot, James Wemyss, whom Charles I made Master Gunner of England in 1638. His invention was a leather gun, a light 1½-pounder consisting of a copper tube strengthened with iron bands covered with a leather skin, a number of which were captured at the battle of Cropredy Bridge.

In October 1642, the crew for a demi-cannon was 3 gunners and 6 mattrosses, while a culverin had a crew of 2 gunners and 4 mattrosses.

A typical Artillery train of the period was quite comprehensive and in 1618 the establishment laid down was:

1 General of Artillery	1 Petardier
1 Lieutenant-General	2 Waggon-makers
1 Comptroller	2 Gabion-makers
1 Commissary	2 Harness-makers
10 Gentlemen of the Ordnance	2 Farriers
25 Conductors	1 Cooper
2 Comptrollers of Fortification	1 Surgeon
1 Master Gunner	1 Surgeon's Mate
136 Gunners	1 Captain of Miners
1 Master Fireworker	25 Miners
2 Conductors of Fireworkers	1 Captain of Pioneers
2 Battery Masters	25 Pioneers
1 Master Carpenter	1 Trench Master
12 Carpenters	1 Waggon Master

During the Civil War the Royalist authorities no doubt found there was a vast gulf between what was desirable and what was financially possible.

Eldred gives these details of the cannon of the time:

	Calibre in inches	Weight in pounds	Length of piece in feet	Weight of charge in pounds	Weight of shot in pounds
Cannon Royal	8	8,000	8	40	63
Cannon	7	7,000	10	34	47
Demi-cannon	6	6,000	12	25	27
Culverin	5	4,000	11	18	15
Demi-culverin	$4\frac{1}{2}$	3,600	10	9	9
Saker	$3\frac{1}{2}$	2,500	$9\frac{1}{2}$	5	$5\frac{1}{4}$
Minion	3	1,500	8	3·5	4
Falcon	$2\frac{3}{4}$	700	6	2·5	$2\frac{1}{4}$
Falconet	2	210	4		$1\frac{1}{4}$
Robinet	$1\frac{1}{4}$	120	3		$\frac{3}{4}$

When the standard was raised at Nottingham on a dismal wet day it met with indifference rather than hostility. Indeed, it seemed for a while that there would be no effective royal army and when,[5] later in the week, the standard blew down, it must have seemed an evil omen to many. A mere 800 horse and 3,000 foot rallied at the call. However, the violence of the sectaries of the Parliamentarian army served the Royalist cause well, for when the Earl of Essex and his men took Worcester on 24 September they indulged in wild religious excesses, while a wave of anti-Catholic feeling swept the south-eastern parts of the country. Possibly it was this ugly facet of Puritanism that settled the minds of many of the waverers and ensured the King a field army.

By the end of September the Royalist forces numbered 2,000 horse and 6,000 foot. A few weeks later these numbers were doubled. By the time the first major battle was fought at Edgehill the King's army had a strength of 2,800 horse,[6] 10,500 foot, 1,000 dragoons and 20 guns – only 1,000 fewer than the Parliamentarian forces from whom they had had to retreat in haste a month previously. Regiments were usually, though not always, raised by an individual. Colonel John Belasyse, for example, took command of a regiment of foot which had been raised at his father's expense. Dutton's regiment and the regiments of the Earl of Lindsey and his son Lord Willoughby D'Eresby were also raised in this way. But in Denbighshire the gentry met and selected one of their number, Sir Thomas Salusbury, as colonel and voted money to raise a regiment of foot, which fought at Edgehill. It was raised valley by valley by the squirarchy of north Wales, and to provide the military expertise they hired George Boncle,[7] a courtier who had been raised as a soldier.

The Cornish repelled the first Roundhead invasion by calling out the *Posse Comitatus*, but these patriots, ready to fight for hearth and home, had no desire to go abroad beyond the Tamar. Thus it came to pass that those worthies, Sir Bevil Grenvile, Sir Nicholas Slanning, William Godolphin, John Trevanion and John Arundel raised the five famous voluntary regiments that carried the day at Launceston, Stratton and Lansdown.

Both sides resorted to the dubious expedient of enlisting prisoners of war. The Cavaliers did so as early as February 1643 when, after the storming of Cirencester, they compelled a number of the Gloucester levies who had defended the place to join them. As the war dragged on it became necessary for both sides to resort to impressment at least to recruit the foot. The constables in each hundred were called upon to provide their quota, although whether either army benefited by this is hard to say.

REFERENCES

1. Clarendon v p. 142.
2. Peacock p. 47.
3. Symonds.
4. Clarendon.
5. ibid. v p. 449.
6. Young, *Edgehill* p. 104.
7. Lieut.-Col. Sir George Boncle, taken prisoner at Naseby. Died later 'of hard usage'.

Chapter Two

Equipping the Men

'Let me excite all to be diligent . . . and willing to get complete
arms . . . considering how ill it was with Israel when there
was not a shield to be found amongst four thousand men.'

Captain Thomas Venn 1672

Possessing the contents of the arsenal at the Tower and sus-
tained by the regular taxation and wealth of London, the
Parliamentarians were at once at a tremendous advantage.
Not only could they train and arm their men, but as a bonus
they also had the services of the London Trained Bands, the
territorial militia trained and paid by the local authorities for
home defence.

Charles had to arm his men as best he might. At York he
looked to the Governor of Hull, Sir John Hotham, to supply
him with the arms deposited there by the disbanded army
that had been sent against the Scots in 1640. These were lost
when Hotham closed the gates and manned the walls against
him. The navy, on which Charles had lavished so much
money, declared for Parliament and blockaded the coast so
that any arms or powder coming to the King from abroad had
to run the gauntlet. Some were successful in this. The
Providence, a fourth-rater of 300 tons, laden with Dutch gunpowder, was captured by the *Mayflower* off Hull. The captain,
with some guile, escaped his guard in the estuary and sailed
the *Providence* into a narrow creek where her deeper draught
opponent dared not follow, and where the King's men
successfully unloaded the cargo.

The commanders on land were, with equal craft, command-
eering the magazines of the local trained bands and searching
the houses of suspected Parliamentarian sympathisers for

arms. In addition to this, many private persons, even of quite humble standing, gave arms, for in those times it was common-place for anyone to possess them. The father of Anthony Wood, the antiquarian, provided 'armour or furniture for one man, viz. a helmet, a back and breast piece, a pike, a musket and other appurtenances'.[1] Captain Robert Millington, who commanded a foot company at Edgehill, presented the King with eighty muskets, while noblemen and gentlemen of quality sent the contents of their own armouries which were 'very mean',[2] according to Clarendon. Captain Richard Atkyns, who raised his troop in 1643, explained: ' . . . within one month I mustered sixty men besides officers and almost all of them well armed. Master [John] Dutton giving me 30 steel backs, breasts and head pieces and two men and horses completely armed.'[3]

However, even with the addition of 800 muskets, 500 pairs of pistols and 200 swords landed in Yorkshire there were not enough weapons for everyone. Three or four hundred of the foot marched only with a cudgel (that is a heavy staff), but the rest were equipped 'with muskets and bags for the powder and pikes; but in the whole body there was not a pikeman that had a corselet and but few musketeers that had a sword'.[4] From a clothing point of view the prospect was better. It is a popular misconception that there was no uniform worn in the Civil War. While the notion of an army dressed in uniforms of a single national colour with regimental facings and other sartorial elegances was still in the future, at least the soldier was issued for the most part with sufficient articles of clothing to give him an appearance uniform with that of his comrades.

The wealthy landowner who recruited his regiment from amongst his tenants would supply them with cap, coat, breeches and woollen stockings, although they might be required to wear their own shoes. The coats were of any hue the donor fancied, blue, white, green, red, orange, grey and even one (Lord Brooke's) in purple! Thomas Bushell, the 'Warden of our Mint and M[aste]r Worker of our Mynes Royall' already mentioned, clothed the King's Lifeguard and three regiments more with 'suites, stockings, shoes and mount-

2. King Charles I: left-hand section of a painting by an unknown artist (see Plate 3) (*National Portrait Gallery*). It seems possible that the painter was William Dobson.

3. Sir Edward Walker: right-hand section of a painting by an unknown
artist (see Plate 2) (*National Portrait Gallery*)

eroes when we were ready to march into the field'. Wood notes that in Oxford on 23 January 1643, a great many of the tailors were set to work in the cutting out of four or five thousand coats for the soldiers, 'which were presently afterward put forth to the taylors here inhabitants, and to strangers within ten miles of Oxford to be made up and finished'.[5] The same source informs us that on 15 July 1643, 'all the common soldiers then at Oxford were new apparelled, some all in red, coates, breeches and mounteroes; and some all in blewe'.[6] It might not be inappropriate to conjecture that this was the completion of the task started in January. Several kinds of hat were issued, the most popular seeming to be the monteroe. This mysterious headgear seems to be in the form of a cap. Corporal Trim, veteran of the siege of Namur (1695), was given one described as being 'scarlet, of a superfine Spanish cloth, dyed in grain and mounted all round with fur, except about four inches in front, which was faced with a light blue, slightly embroidered'. Another description given by one Thomas Ellwood seems to give it a brim, for he states

A military conversation!

that he wore 'a large montero cap of black velvet, the skirt of which being turned up in folds, looked somewhat above the then common garb of a Quaker'. Perhaps there were different styles of the same cap. Definitely a cheaper sort of headwear was the Monmouth cap. In 1642 they were selling at 23 shillings per dozen. Symonds, writing from Bewdley in 1644, tells of the manufacture of these caps: 'First they are knit, then they mill them, then block them, then they work them with tassels, then they sheer them.'[7] One wonders if this could be a sort of stocking cap with a long tail and tassel hanging over one ear, as it seems that by 1742 it was sold chiefly to seamen. Possibly the soldiers preferred the broad-brimmed felt hat, which we picture when thinking of the Royalists, as this was useful in protecting the wearer from both sun and rain.

As a necessary extra to their clothing the soldiers also received a 'snapsack' (the modern term 'knapsack' is probably a corruption of this) made of leather or canvas, and the musketeers were issued with bags for their powder and bandoliers from which dangled their cartridges, sometimes known as the 'twelve apostles'. The sergeants and officers, receiving no general issue, could be expected to dress rather differently from the soldiers. There were no badges of rank, the sergeant being recognised by the halberd he carried, while the general richness of the officer's attire, as well as the gold-fringed sash round his waist, was sufficient indication of his status. If further indication was required the foot officer was armed with a partisan.

In 1642 the universally accepted colour of the Parliament was the orange tawny hue originating with the Earl of Essex. Roundhead officers wore sashes of this colour and the men often wore orange tawny hat bands.

ARMS

The fully accoutred pikeman of the period was heavily laden. He carried a pike 16 or 18 feet long, steel shod with a steel spear point head and a sword. He wore a helmet with ear protectors, a thick leather buff coat and over this a breast and back plate, while loosely attached to the former were metal plates called tassets which reached almost to the knees and protected the thighs and upper legs. The schedule of prices of arms fixed by Charles I in 1632 established the cost of a pikeman's armour thus:[8]

	£	s	d
The breast		5	6
The backe		4	6
The tassets		5	0
The comb'd headpiece lyned		4	6
The gorget lined		2	6
The total	£1	2	0

Before commenting on the cheapness of the outfit by today's standards one should remember that the purchasing power of the pound in the seventeenth century was at least twenty times greater than today.

In practice, in the early stages in 1642 and 1643 at least, we have seen that commanders were pleased to have a proportion of their men armed at all, let alone in accordance with a laid down standard. The predominance of pike over musket was caused by the ease with which a blacksmith could turn out pike heads and the shortage of muskets. Many of the rustics were probably armed with pitchforks, flails and scythes, as at Sedgemoor, until the fortunes of war placed captured weapons in their hands.

The Musketeers
These were armed with matchlocks though a few might possess firelocks or snaphances – early versions of the flintlock. The matchlock was over 5 feet long and quite heavy, so it was supported in the aiming position by a rest. This was an ash stick with a metal-shod base and a U-shaped retaining arm at the top. While a musket ball would travel 400 yards it was inaccurate over 40. The loading process was slow and cumbersome. First the pan was filled with fine priming powder then the musketeer pushed the cap off the charge holder and poured an exact measured amount of powder into the barrel.

This was rammed home with the ball by a wooden ramrod or scourer which was carried for convenience in a recess under the barrel. One end of the smouldering slow match was clipped onto the serpentine, a curved arm secured to the side of the stock. The musketeer blew on the end of the match to make it glow. The piece was now ready to fire. It will be seen that, even with an expert, a firing rate greater than one round every five minutes was not possible. However, although encumbered with spare lengths of slow match, powder horns, bandoliers and a sword, the musketeers were far more mobile than the pikemen, for they wore no defensive armour, their headgear being the broad-brimmed hat, montero or Monmouth cap.

The very nature of the arms of the foot dictated that they should form up in a deep formation with the pikes in the centre and the musketeers on the flanks. Thus the musketeers could give a rolling fire and could, in case of attack, shelter behind the pikemen, although they could (and often did) club the muskets and lay about them.

The Dragoons

According to General Monck,[8] the dragoons were to be equipped with snaphance or flintlock muskets, which could be fired from the saddle. These were a great deal more reliable and successful than the matchlock described above, as well as being more expensive; they eliminated the slow match in their operation, substituting a method of producing sparks by friction. The dragoon was to have a belt to hang the musket on, a pair of bandoliers and a good long tuck (sword) with a belt. In general they much resembled the foot. The officers and men of the Artillery also resembled the foot, despite their lack of arms, although at the siege of Lichfield in March 1643 Rupert's men had pole-axes and the wheelwrights swords. The carters, being civilians, would presumably wear their own clothes.

The Royalist Cavalry

They were mostly gentlemen and their outdoor servants who

had spent their lives in the saddle. Until the advent of Cromwell and his Ironsides they were superior to the general run of Parliamentarian cavalry. They probably took the field in the clothes they normally wore for riding, supplemented with whatever armour was available – ideally a buff coat, with a breast and back plate and pot helmet to complete the outfit; while a pair of pistols and sword were the appropriate arms. Clarendon, however, describes the real state of affairs: 'The officers had their full desire if they were able to produce old backs and breasts and pots with pistols or carbines for their two or three front ranks and swords for the rest, themselves having gotten besides their pistols and carbines, a short pole axe.'[10] But even these were sufficient to lend a troop a certain air of uniformity and some of them were very well turned out, particularly the King's Lifeguard who, much to their indignation, were called the 'Troop of Show'.

Troopers were seemingly issued with cloaks or coats. Prince Rupert received a letter from Sir Thomas Dallison that he had some hundreds of yards of red cloth 'which may make cloaks or coats for your Highness' regiment of horse'. A rarity in the Royalist forces was the three-quarters armour of the cuirassier, where the armour came to the knee. Some individuals may have worn it but certainly no units. Sir Arthur Heselrig, however, on the Parliamentarian side, did equip his men in this fashion. Clarendon has left us this record of them: 'They were so completely armoured that they were called by the other side the regiment of lobsters because of their bright iron shells by which they were covered, being perfect cuirassiers, and were the first to be so armed on either side.'[11]

Each troop was entitled to two trumpeters. These were dressed in a singular fashion, without armour and with curious hanging sleeves. The attire of the senior officers may be judged from their portraits. While many chose to be painted in their battle attire of buff coat, breast plate and gorget, others proclaimed their quality by wearing their best suits of armour, like Sir Richard Willys whose armour in Dobson's portrait is richly decorated with bands of gold. One might think that such ostentation was an open invitation to

the enemy to single the wearer out. Evidently Prince Rupert
thought this, for at Brentford he 'took off his scarlet coat
which was very rich and gave it to his man and buckled on
his arms and put a grey coat over it so that he might not be
discovered'.[12] On the day of Edgehill the King wore a black
velvet cloak lined with ermine and a steel cap covered with
velvet.

COLOURS

The idea of forming soldiers into companies was a medieval
one, but the notion of forming companies into regiments did
not occur until the sixteenth century when armies were first
organised in this fashion. There is nothing new in rallying
men on to a standard or flag, but the idea of company colours
capable of telling the initiated the status of the person at its
head and colour coded to tell also the name of the regiment,
was novel in the time of the Civil War. The colonel who commanded the regiment chose the background colour for his
regiment and his flag (or colour, as the infantry flags were
called) was plainly of this colour without any addition. The
lieutenant-colonel[13] had the same background but with a
St George's cross in the top corner next to the staff. The
major added 'a little stream blazant', coming at an angle from
the bottom-right hand corner of the cross. The captain's
colour had the St George's cross and the background but with
a device chosen by the colonel, often from his armorial bear-
ings: one for the first captain, two for the second, three for the
third and so on. These colours were of painted taffeta and
were made large enough (6½ feet by 6½ feet) to be seen through
the smoke of battle or from a distance. Captain Thomas Venn,
quoting from Gervase Markham's *Souldiers Accidence* (1625)
tells us the meanings of the various colours, metals and furs
used in the designs:

Black	'Signifieth Wisdom and Sobriety'
Yellow (Gold)	'Betokeneth honour or height of spirit'
White (Silver)	'Signifieth innocence or purity of conscience'
Red	'Justice or noble worthy anger'

Blue	'Faith, constancy and truth'
Green	'Good hope'
Purple	'Fortitude with discretion'
Tawny	'Signifieth merit'
Ermine	'A rich fur with curious spots signifieth religion or holiness'

The dragoon's guidons and the cavalry's standards were much smaller; two standards surviving from the period in the church at Bromsberrow measure 2 feet by 2 feet, but these follow the same rules only in so far as the coloured background is concerned. Most of the standards bore mottoes or devices of a political or religious nature on both sides. Occasionally one comes across colours that do not follow this rule, and perhaps the explanation is that they are of an earlier pattern still in use. The following descriptions are of standards taken at Marston Moor:

A black cornet with black and yellow fringe and a sword reaching out from a cloud with the motto '*Terribilis ut acies ordinata*' (Terrible as a battle line drawn up).

A black cornet with a black fringe and in the middle three crowns gilded with the motto '*Quarta perennis erit*' (The quarter will be eternal).

A blue cornet with a crown towards the top and a mitre beneath it, with the Parliament painted on the side and the motto '*Nolite tangere christos meos*' (Touch not my anointed ones).

A willow green standard with the 'portraiture' of a man holding in one hand a sword and in the other a knot with the motto 'This shall untie it'.

The ubiquitous drill book, the bane of the soldier's life, was present, even at this stage of the army's history, in all its complexity and elaboration. All that is needed is a modern drill sergeant to bring it right up to date!

ROYALIST UNIFORMS

Regiment	Colour	Source
1. King's Lifeguard	red	Richard Symond's
2. Queen's Lifeguard	red	manuscript notebook,
3. Prince Rupert's Firelocks	red	B M Harl. 986
4. Sir Allan Apsley	red	
5. Colonel Edward Hopton	red	
6. Prince Charles (CO Sir Michael Woodhouse)	blue	Shrewsbury Borough Records. Billeting document of 1643 refers
7. Lord Hopton	blue	As 1
8. Charles Gerrard	blue	
9. Sir Thomas Lunsford	blue	As 6
10. Henry Lunsford	blue	
11. Prince Rupert	blue	
12. Sir Ralph Dutton	white	Sir Edward Walker's
13. Sir Stephen Hawkins	white	*Historical Discourses* p. 92
14. Lord Percy	white	As 1
15. Marquis of Newcastle's	white	*Life of ... Duke of Newcastle*, ed. C. H. Firth, 1886, p. 79
16. Colonel Thomas Pinchbeck	grey	As 1
17. Colonel Sir Henry Bard	grey	
18. Earl of Northampton	green	Washbourn, *Bibliotheca Gloucestrensis* vol. 1 p. 229
19. Colonel Robert Broughton	green	Diary of Richard
20. Colonel Henry Tillier	green	Symonds, Camden Society 1859, p. 255
21. Colonel Talbot	yellow	As 1
22. Sir Charles Vavasour	yellow	*Memoirs of Edward*
23. Sir Matthew Appleyard	yellow	*Ludlow*, Ed. C. H. Firth, 1894, vol.1 p. 72

	Regiment	Colour	Source
24.	Sir John Paulet	yellow	As 6
25.	Sir Thomas Blackwall	black	

PARLIAMENTARY UNIFORMS

	Regiment	Colour	Source
1.	Lord Robartes*	red	C. H. Firth,
2.	Sir Thomas Fairfax	Red lined blue	*Cromwell's Army* p. 232–3
3.	Denzil Holles*	red	
4.	Edward Montague	red lined white	
5.	Norfolk Regiment	red	Royal Commission Hist. Monuments, *Newark-on-Trent Civil War Siege Works* p. 96
6.	Essex Regiments	Red lined blue	As 1
7.	Earl of Stamford*	blue	John Washbourn, *Bibliotheca Gloucestrensis* vol. 1 p. 229
8.	Lord Saye and Sele	blue	As 1
9.	Sir William Constable*	blue	
10.	Sir Henry Cholmley*	blue	Young
11.	Sir William Springate	white?	
12.	Earl of Manchester	Green lined red	As 1 (1643)
13.	Sir John Merrick*	Grey	Warburton, vol. 1 p. 428
14.	Sir John Gell	grey	Hutchinson, '*Memoirs . . . Col. Hutchinson*', ed. C. H. Firth, 1885

Note. * denotes members of Essex's 1642 army.

	Regiment	Colour	Source
15.	Thomas Ballard*	grey	As 1
16.	Simon Rugeley	grey	Pennington/Roots, *The Committee of Stafford 1643–5*, 1957
17.	John Hampden*	green	As 1
18.	Samuel Jones	green	Adair, *Court Martial Papers of Sir William Waller's Army 1644*, p. 64
19.	Lord Brooke	purple	As 1
20.	Thomas Grantham	russet	Wood vol. 1 pp. 66–7

Note. * denotes members of Essex's 1642 army.

REFERENCES

1. Wood 1 p. 53.
2. Clarendon vi p. 73.
3. Atkyns/Gwyn p. 7.
4. Clarendon vi p. 73.
5. Wood 1 p. 83–4.
6. op. cit. p. 103.
7. Symonds' diary p. 14.
8. Grose ii p. 335.
9. Monck p. 27.
10. Clarendon vi p. 73.
11. ibid. vii p. 104.
12. Warburton ii p. 62.
13. Venn p. 186.

Chapter Three

On the March

'To most regiments there is allowed two waggons for the baggage
and ammunition . . . besides other carriages
which more concern the soldiers victual . . . '
Lieutenant-Colonel Richard Elton   1659

As a result of the advent of good roads, shorter working hours
and the comparative cheapness of transport, it is possible that
we know our country more intimately than any previous
generation. Even in the late nineteenth century the common
man was a fixture, his rare outings confined to the distance a
waggonette could travel and return in a day. In the seventeenth century few, besides the nobleman or the travelling
tradesman, had any knowledge of other parts of the country.
The crude roads, little better than tracks, deep in mud, and
the dependence on the land for a living, anchored most
people in one spot. Let the reader who is unduly critical of the
apparently blundering progress of the armies of those times
bear in mind the handicaps under which the general officers
worked. Lacking any of the forms of communication we take
for granted, with maps scarce and of little military use, their
task was formidable. Not only how but where to transport
their army must have been a nightmare, and often the staff
could have had little more than a general idea of the enemy's
position and even less of his numbers and disposition.

Before Edgehill it is apparent that Charles and his staff
were uncertain how to engage Essex, who then lay at
Worcester. Should they, the Council argued, march on the
town, knowing it to be of Royalist sympathies, or should they
march on London, being certain that their opponents would
have to block their path? Those who favoured the former

course maintained that 'no time should be lost in coming to a battle because the longer it was deferred the stronger the Earl would grow by the supplies that were sent every day from London'.[1] Eventually, however, it was decided that they should adopt the latter course. In the country around Worcester the ground was too enclosed to allow cavalry to operate freely, and as the King had great faith in the ability of the horse to win for him 'the other way was felt to be fitter for the engagement'.[2] Any advance was bound to be tedious for the speed was naturally governed by the slowest arm, in this case the Ordnance.

The following table gives some idea of what was needed to move some of the guns of the period. Note the estimated man-power required if horses or oxen were not available.

Type	Weight	No. of men	No. of horses
Cannon Royal	71·5 cwt	90	16
Cannon	62 cwt	70	12
Demi-cannon	53·5 cwt	60	10
Culverin	41 cwt	50	8
Demi-culverin	22·3 cwt	36	7
Saker and Drake	14·3 cwt	24	5
Minion	10·5 cwt	20	4
Falcon	6·2 cwt	16	2

In time the Royalist army was to be better organised, but the mind boggles at the thought of that army of amateurs endeavouring to get under way with the minority of professional soldiers probably tearing their hair in an excess of frustration. It cannot be stated with certainty that patrols were sent out ahead of the army at this early stage of its development. Certainly they should have been, and as the commanders became more experienced and the men soldiers, rather than civilians-in-arms, it became a commonplace.

The army was marshalled in brigades or 'tertias' – a new form – commanded by the lowest rank of general officer. It was of an indeterminate size although at Edgehill the foot brigades averaged about 2,000 men. At the head or 'van' there were two brigades of cavalry followed by a brigade of

Making friends with the local inhabitants

foot. After them came King Charles on horseback with his Lifeguard bearing the Banner Royal and surrounded by his Council of War, which consisted of generals, peers, ministers and field officers. Next in line would come another infantry brigade, and following them the ponderous body of the artillery train, protected by musketeers armed with snaphance muskets which were a great deal safer near powder, requiring, as we have seen, no smouldering slow match to fire the charge. Although the battle plan of Naseby shows a neat array of uniform four-wheel waggons with canvas tilts and well packed loads, one may assume that every wheeled vehicle for miles around had been commandeered or bought to transport the artillery accessories before Edgehill. As many professional carters as could be persuaded to drive the carts were promised sixpence a day when they were not driving and one shilling when they were. As we have seen, the guns had no limbers, and it took six or eight heavy cart-horses, harnessed in tandem, to pull the field guns through the mire. So they were in great demand, and agents for both sides were busily buying up all beasts available, particularly at the markets where the value of a waggon and seven good horses was set at £82. If horses were not available oxen were used but always with a view to changing to horses when possible.

Some idea of the vast quantity and range of materials needed to supply the needs of the King's army may be gained from a catalogue of 'the state of his Majesty's magazine in His Highnesses train of Artillery' made at Wardington in October 1642. They include over a thousand round shot for various calibres of cannon, 1,200 rests for muskets, 2 tons of musket shot, 500 shovels and spades, 100 pickaxes, 10 wheelbarrows, 100 axes, besides pigs of lead, bars of iron, tents, planks, ropes and tools. Having succeeded in packing these and harnessing up, the train was formed up into three divisions as follows:[3]

1st Division:	The Captain and his pioneers
	Materials (shovels, spades, hatchets, pickaxes, etc.)
	Horse harness
	Hurdles
	The Ordnance
	Budge barrels, cartouches, etc.
	Gynnes, mitches, etc.
	The lord general's waggon
	The lieutenant-general's waggon
	Principal officers' waggons
	Iron shot and case shot
	Match
	Powder
	Materials (smith's tools and tents)
2nd Division:	For the foot and horse
	Powder
	Match
	Musket carbine and pistol shot
3rd Division:	The standing magazine

Besides this there was much personal baggage, for the Court, for the King, the princes and generals and other high-ranking officers. There were the coaches that would accompany the noblemen even here (Essex's coach was taken at Edgehill), and the spare horses for the cavalry and staff—even the foot officers had quite an astonishing number either for riding or as pack animals. Then there would be the vehicles for the victuallers, traders and a whole host of other persons who had a commercial interest in the army, including a good percentage of 'light ladies of pleasure'. The tremendous number of waggons that proceeded on that march to the first battle of the war may be judged from the fact that the King detached fifty-seven waggons as a bye train to support Sir Nicholas Byron's brigade who were charged with the task of taking Banbury. The rear would be brought up by yet another two brigades of cavalry.

Our unpredictable weather plays havoc with travel even today. In the autumn in the seventeenth century its effects were devastating. On 24 September, Wharton notes, 'the rain continued all day and the way so base that we went up to the ankles in thick clay'.[4] It takes little imagination to visualise the scene as the army, spread out over five or more miles of road, floundered and squelched along. The foot, burdened with musket or pike and other items, would soon be mired up to the waist, while the carters would be cracking their whips over the straining backs of the horses with men tugging on the wheels to extricate themselves from the morass. How many volunteers brought face to face with the realities of the service must have cursed the impulse that led them to join their Squire for 'King and Country', or the canting, snuffle-nosed preacher who had persuaded them that their duty was to 'God and Parliament'. For in describing the Royalist progression one has also described the progression of the Parliamentarian army.

It took the King ten days to move from Shrewsbury to near Banbury, a distance of less than 100 miles. By the standards of the time this was fair marching: Essex on his march from Worcester to Kineton only averaged 8¾ miles per day. Much time was consumed each day billeting the men out in the villages in a wide area on the route of march, for the weather was bitter and the tents few. So foul were the conditions that on 30 September en route to Hereford a soldier died 'by reason of the rain, snow and extremity of cold'.[5] Thus the lengthy task of finding quarters for the night and reassembling in the morning was a necessity, if a large proportion of the men were not to be casualties from exposure. Naturally the King and his immediate subordinates were sheltered under the roof of the nearest great house. On the night of 12 October Charles stayed at the house of Sir William Chancie at Edgecote, Prince Rupert was five miles away with Lord Spencer at Wormleighton, and the lord general, Lord Lindsey, was at Culworth. The Prince's quartermasters arrived at Wormleighton, just as those of the Earl of Essex did. However, it would seem that the Royalists recovered from their surprise first for they captured the Roundheads and 'we had intelligence where ye Enemy was'.[6] The end of the march was in sight and the end of all things for many of the marchers.

REFERENCES

1. Clarendon VI p. 76.
2. ibid.
3. Roy p. 154.
4. Wharton was a sergeant in Holles's regiment (see Bibliography).
5. Wharton.
6. Prince Rupert's diary.

Chapter Four

Oxford—Court, Fortress and Headquarters

When first I went to Oxford, fully there intent
To study learned science I went.
Instead of Logicke, Physicke, school converse
I did attend the armed troops of Mars.
Instead of books I sword, horse, pistols bought
And on the field I for degrees then fought.

Anthony Cooper, *Stratologia*, 1662[1]

Oxford at the start of the Civil War was, by seventeenth-century standards, quite a large city. A census taken on 7 June 1643 shows a total of 3,320 males aged between 16 and 60, so that a reasonable estimation of the entire population might be assumed to be of the order of 10,000 souls. Hollar's map of 1643 shows that most of them were contained within the ancient walls, although a certain amount of building had commenced beyond the gates. In addition there were the suburbs of St Thomas's to the west, Holywell to the north-east and St Clement's to the east over the river Cherwell. The official description of the place at this time was 'the city and university of Oxford', which shows how, in the official mind as in fact, the city was split into two factions, the tradesmen and townfolk versus the University and its servants. The animosity between the two was bitter and age old, so that it was almost inevitable that with the well known Royalist sympathies of the University, the city would be bound to take the opposite side whether from conviction or just from habit. For a short time the expectations of the citizens were high.

Parliamentarian troops under Lord Saye occupied Oxford, disarming the University and distributing the arms amongst the citizens; but their triumph was short-lived, for on or about 20 October 1642 the city was evacuated. While Saye had been in occupation, in addition to searching the colleges for arms he had looked for hidden plate, of which he found a quantity.

After Edgehill the citizens' hopes were finally dashed. Thereafter for four years the city became Charles's chief garrison, the seat of his Court, Mint and Government. On 29 October, Wood tells us,[2] towards evening, the King, with Princes Charles, James, Maurice and Rupert and their triumphant army, entered the city by the north gate bearing with them a large number of captured Parliamentarian colours. The Mayor and townsfolk, having no option, met the King and made a loyal speech of welcome, which he un-doubtedly recognised for the hypocrisy it was. The royal party were housed at Christ Church and there they were met by Dr Richard Gardiner, who made another speech (of the sincerity of which the King could have been in no doubt) while 'the University stood'. One of Charles's first acts on taking up residence was to disarm the citizens. On 4 November a cart-load of muskets and another of powder were removed from the Guildhall and lodged 'at the Schoole, in the uppermost room of the Schoole tower by such as the King's councell of warre had appointed'.[3] With the citizens' ability to resist thus negated, their thoughts turned, very naturally, to making the most of a bad situation. Their task, as the King saw it, was to provide for the wants of the Court and garrison. Being men of business the tradesmen saw no reason why they should not be well paid for their services. Once they had accustomed them-selves to the facts of military occupations, no doubt life went on much as before, but with an added impetus and additional profit.

THE MINT

One of Charles's oft quoted remarks is that 'money is the nerves of war', and indeed one cannot quarrel with it. The coins of the reign were the Unite (£1), the half-Unite (50p), the Angel (37½p) in gold; and the crown, half-crown, shilling, sixpence, threepence, twopence and one penny in silver. Under the Stuarts the copper farthing was introduced. Coins were still made by the ancient, time-consuming way of hammering by hand, although primitive machines had been made as early as the time of Elizabeth I to produce coins by the mill and screw method. This forerunner of today's presses was not popular, however, particularly with the moneyers who saw in them the diminution of their privileges. In the reign of Charles I only two issues of machine-made coins were struck, although these were such fine examples that further issues might well have been made but for the war. Although the main Mint was in the Tower of London, there were also lesser mints. With the loss of London the King at first used the mint at York to coin money to pay the army and later he removed the Aberystwyth branch complete to Shrewsbury. The product of this mint is distinguished by a device containing the three feathers of the Prince of Wales's crest, and it utilised silver extracted from the lead ores of that country. The King entered Oxford, as we have seen, in October 1642 and sometime before the end of the year he decided to make it his permanent headquarters. On 15 December 1642 he issued a proclamation establishing the Royal Mint at Oxford. A line of carts arrived in the city on 2 January 1643 containing the Shrewsbury Mint and a good store of ore, as well as some of Prince Rupert's goods. No time was lost in setting it up in New Inn Hall, which was empty and deserted at the time. Thomas Bushell, the Warden and Master Worker, and Sir William Parkhurst were put in charge and to them also fell the task of collecting raw material to make into coins. This was achieved by requisitioning the college plate and that of certain private individuals. The King[4] sent out what we might call a circular letter couched in persuasive terms:

Trusty and well beloved wee greete you well . . . we cannot doubt that you will take all occassions to expres [your love] and as we are ready to sell or engage any of our land, so have we melted down our plate, for the paiment of our army. . . . We do hereby desire that you lend us all such plate of what kind whatsoever that belongs to your colledge, promising to see the same repaid to you . . . for assure yourselves wee shall never let persons, of whom wee have so great care, suffer for their affection, but shall take speciall order for the repaiment. . . . And we assure ourselfe of your willingness to assist us herein. . . . Wee shall ever remember this particular service to your advantage.

There seems to have been little opposition to this seventeenth-century compulsory purchase order for on 20 January there arrived 1,856 lb 16 oz 19 dwt of plate at the Mint made up as follows:[5]

	lb	oz	dwt
The Cathedral Church of Christ	172	3	14
Jesus College	86	11	5
Oriel	82	0	19
Queen's	193	3	1
Lincoln	47	2	5
University	61	6	5
Brasenose	121	2	15
St Mary Magdalen	296	6	15
All Souls	253	1	19
Balliol	41	4	0
Merton	79	11	10
Trinity	174	7	10
Exeter	246	5	1

It was not to be supposed that, even with the known Royalist sympathies of the colleges, the response would be 100 per cent. Exeter quibbled, protesting that it was contrary to its statutes to part with the plate, but soon found that the letter couched as a request was in actual fact an order, and on 2 February delivered 246 lb to the officers. St John's tried a different tack and sent a sum of £800 in lieu of the plate, wishing to preserve the memory of the benefactors by retaining the silver. It was all to no avail. The King kept the money and still demanded the plate. Later on, when the Royal exchequer was getting low, silver was substituted for gold in the unite and half-unite, while a new coin was produced, the large gold Oxford £3 piece. Corpus Christi has now the best collection of pre-Civil War plate.

The metal was not only used for coins. The first medals were made and presented—not a general issue, it is true, but for recognition of service in the field. Sir John Smith, who saved the Banner Royal at Edgehill, was awarded 'a large medal in Gold with the King's picture on the one side and the Banner on the other which he always wore . . . in a large green watered ribbon on his shoulders'.[6] It was Bushell's idea that a medal should be struck for the forlorn hope, which was doubtless highly prized—the forlorn hope being a strong body of musketeers stationed about 100 yards forward of the first battle line, hence in a position of some peril. Perhaps it would not be wrong to compare it with the modern Distinguished Conduct Medal. Thomas Rawlins, a pupil of the noted medal engraver Nicholas Briot was responsible for the design of these as well as the Kineton Medal, the Bristol Medal and others. The work of the Oxford Mint is a fine example of what a nucleus of highly skilled men can achieve.

THE CASTLE AND FORTIFICATIONS

The map by Agas (1578) gives a good idea of the form of the castle as it probably appeared at the time of the Civil War. It was almost circular, with a mighty three-storeyed tower on a mound and a large tower at each angle, one in particular where the front might seem weakest being a huge edifice of great strength. The walls were battlemented and the whole surrounded by a wide moat into which the river had apparently been admitted. The main entrance was through the south-east tower via a high wooden bridge. The insertion of a small bridge over the Thames immediately opposite a three-storeyed tower with a building attached seems to make the provision of a postern gate there very probable. The absence of any residential buildings in the bailey is explained by the

The Figures of the three famous Batteries, which were raised by Spinola at the Siege of Breda.

Figures of the three famous batteries raised by Spinola at
the siege of Breda (*Royal Commission on
Historical Monuments, England*)

For the raiſing of Fortifications, we muſt obſerve what Figures are capable of Regular Fortification, and what are uncapable ; which are termed Irregular.

Regular Fortifications are ſuch formes or figures, which containe in them Angles ſufficiently equall, and capable for the direct anſwering one to another ; ſixe points being the leaſt that may be admitted , and ſo upwards : all figures under, are termed Irregular ; as the figure *Pentagon* conſiſting of Five points , the Foure-ſquare , the Triangle, &c.

We will firſt begin with Irregular-figures uſed in Fortification ; of which the *Pentagon* is the beſt, in regard it hath more capacity in it , than the Foure-ſquare, or Triangle , or Halfe-Moones, &c. The forme of this Figure hath five points, by reaſon of five Lines that divide the Circumference in five equall parts, as by this Figure appeares.

The next Irregular Figure, is the Foure ſquare ; and is capable of foure Bulworkes, upon each point one ; and is tearmed a *Skonſe*, as the Figure demonſtrates.

The next Irregular Figure is the Triangle, being farre inferiour in ſtrength to the former, in regard it is capable but of three Bulworks, upon each point one ; as the Figure demonſtrates.

The next Irregular Figure, is the Horne-worke ; and is moſt proper for the lodging of men in it, and for the ſecuring of the principall walles and Bulworks of a Fort, from the ruining of the ſhot.

All Forts framed without Bulworks, are eyther *Redoubts*, or halfe Moones; of which are divers faſhions : as firſt, a quadrangle Redoubt.

The next is a Triangle Redoubt.

A

Figures used in fortification. (*Royal Commission on Historical Monuments, England*)

fact that all the towers were inhabited, as the windows plainly show.

The label Castle Prison shows plainly the depths to which this once proud stronghold had been reduced, as does the grim scaffold left permanently in place in the bailey. During the Civil War it was again used for military purposes, troops and prisoners being billeted there with seeming impartiality. The prisoners were inclined to regard their accommodation as rather less than satisfactory. On 13 May the House of Commons debated a petition from them alleging 'violence to person, extortion, denial of rations, beds, access to friends and surgeons to dress their wounds. Lodging in heaps not only on the ground, upon bare boards, and in loathsome and filthy dungeons'. The chief object of their complaint was, 'one Smith, a provost marshal in the King's army'. The House threatened retaliation against Royalist prisoners if these matters were not speedily remedied and asked Essex to acquaint the King with this resolution. The King's allowance was sixpence per day per prisoner and the complaint was that they were only receiving $1\frac{1}{2}$ pence per day. Obviously the prison officers were lining their pockets if the prisoners' complaint was true. Captain William Smith, the provost marshal in question, wrote a petition to the King, now preserved among the Harleian manuscripts, in extenuation of his conduct. He was not supplied with the necessary guards, and those that were supplied deserted him or were negligent. He was without a deputy and compelled to work single-handed. Without wages for eight months he had been called upon to keep twenty-eight horses for Prince Maurice's dragoons all winter and received allowance for only eight. To complete his catalogue of woes he complains that owing to the nature of his appointment he was treated with disrespect. Whatever the truth of the matter may have been, he was superseded. Edmund Ludlow,[7] who was a prisoner in the castle for three weeks awaiting exchange, has much to say about the conditions and particularly about Smith. It is obvious that the threat of reprisals by the Westminster Parliament had a beneficial effect on the prisoners' welfare.

With the rivers Isis and Cherwell protecting the city on all sides but the north, the fortifying of Oxford was not difficult. Work was started[8] on a bulwark at St Giles which was prolonged through the New Parks. A new order required all civilians between 16 and 60 to attend one day a week under the direction of a Colonel Lloyd. The working day was to be from 6 a.m. to 11 a.m. and from 1 p.m. to 6 p.m. There was no pay for the work which was to be 'for the love of his Majesty'. The citizens had already shown their sentiments with regard to Charles and their attitude to the whole affair was one of sullen antagonism. More metal was requisitioned for the war effort, not silver plate this time but peals of bells from many of the churches to be cast into cannon in St Mary's College. On 13 March 1643 the Governor, Sir Jacob Astley, caused trees in the vicinity of St Clement's to be cut down to improve the field of fire. Wood tells us how in April the banks of the Cherwell were cut to 'overflow Christchurch medes and Cowley landes above Milham bridge . . . for the defence of the cittie'.[9]

On 21 July the fortifications were nearing completion, but the antagonism of the citizens had slowed the work down and the King was forced to make another stringent proclamation. Everybody in the University had to work one day on them or pay a fine of 12 pence. Even noblemen, privy councillors and women were not exempt. This had the effect of ensuring completion. All the time the city was in Royalist hands the works were added to, but it was done at great cost, mainly to the inhabitants of both the city and the University. A virtual dictatorship was established, and when Sir Arthur Aston was Governor he was empowered to enforce obedience 'by committing to prison all refractory persons or by any such punishment as these Commissioners . . . shall think fit, and is used in time of war or siege'. The report of Fairfax's Council of War on 3 May assessed the fortifications in their final form:

. . . accounted a place of great strength before, yet now [the city] was made incomparably stronger than before . . . By making locks at Clement's Bridge they had made it [the

Cherwell] overflow the meadows – so that the city to the extent of three parts of it . . . was surrounded by water to be unapproachable . . . this line above the city (newly finished) was found to be very high, having many strong bulwarks so regularly flanking one another that nothing could be more exactly done . . . Upon the outside of the ditch round the line it was strongly palisaded, and without that again, were digged several pits in the ground so that a single foeman could not without difficulty approach the brink of the ditch.

When the King came to Oxford he brought with him 27 pieces of ordnance; at the surrender of Oxford there were found 38 pieces – 26 being of brass – and 70 barrels of gunpowder. Since the mill at Osney was set to produce gunpowder and, as we have seen, ordnance was produced at St Mary's College, the excess may indicate the degree of industry that the King and his officers induced. Twelve guns had been lost at Naseby, but many others had been captured, and some had been imported.

THE PARLIAMENT

A strange situation evolved in which there were two Parliaments sitting, both declaring themselves the only true and representative body and roundly declaring the other to be guilty of high treason and an illegal assembly. Much of their early activities during the war was issuing proclamations against each other. On 20 June 1643 the King opened the paper battle with a broadside which bade all members of Parliament join him at Oxford. All members who remained at Westminster were guilty of high treason. The Roundhead reply to this was to threaten that all members of the House of Commons who departed the cities of London and Westminster without leave would have their estates sequestrated for deserting the service of the Commonwealth in time of imminent danger. Other retaliatory proclamations followed and the Oxford Parliament had its first meeting, which was in Christ Church Hall, on 22 January 1644, and was addressed

An impoverished Royalist family in poor lodgings at Oxford

briefly by Charles. Then the members adjourned to separate chambers, the Lords (of whom there were 44) to the 'Upper Schools' and the Commons (118) to the 'Great Convocation Hall'. That a good proportion more joined the King is shown by a list issued in 1646 noting 83 Lords and 175 Commons. However, it must not be assumed that this was a subservient body subscribing to the King's every wish without demur: in the King's cabinet captured at Naseby there was a 'top secret' letter to the Queen in which he describes the House as 'the place of base and mutinous motions', and the members as 'our mongrel Parliament'. Little is known of the day-to-day transactions of the Oxford Parliament as, before the surrender of the city to Sir Thomas Fairfax, the lords of the Privy Council caused 'all the books and papers of Parliamentary proceedings to be burned'.

THE GARRISON

The hard core of the garrison consisted of regular soldiers of the 'Oxford Army'. Their members, and indeed their constituent regiments, were never static, changing as the exigencies of the service demanded. On 9 December 1642 they consisted of the Guard (red coats),[10] Colonel Charles Gerrard's regiment (blue coats), Sir William Pennyman's (probably blue coats), Sir Ralph Dutton's (white coats) and the Lifeguard Horse. Just over a year later in a muster in New Parks (13 February 1644) the garrison consisted of the King's and Queen's Lifeguards (both red coats), Lord Percy's regiment (white coats), Colonel Pinchbeck's (grey coats) and Charles Gerrard's.[11] The necessity of protecting the royal headquarters meant that numbers of seasoned troops were bottled up when they might be performing valuable field service elsewhere. To combat this two regiments of auxiliaries were formed. One was named, strangely enough, the Scholars and Strangers, and was commanded by the Earl of Dover. That there was a certain class consciousness about the two constituents of the force was seen by the fact that the Scholars were permitted to form themselves into separate companies. The other force was made up of gentlemen from the Inns of Court who had followed the King from London, and was commanded by Lord Littleton. In addition to these auxiliaries there was a city regiment formed from the townsfolk. Membership of this was, as in the case of the college plate, a polite form of blackmail. Although it was said to be voluntary, non-volunteers were held to be disaffected and asked to leave the city. In December 1643 the officers of this regiment were as follows:

Colonel	Sir Nicholas Selwyn
Lieutenant-Colonel	Mr Thomas Smyth (alderman and mayor)
Sergeant-Major	Mr Hall

1st Captain	Mr Leonard Bowman (mercer and alderman)
2nd Captain	Mr Peter Langston (barrister-at-law)
3rd Captain	Mr Henry Stephens (wagon master general)

The Parliament estimated that the strength of the garrison on 6 June 1644 was 1,500 regular soldiers, 2 regiments of auxiliaries and 300 horse. When Fairfax held his Council of War on 9 June 1646, he assessed the strength as 4,000 foot, 300 horse and 3 regiments of auxiliaries. This latter figure was probably exaggerated to make the final surrender of Oxford seem a greater achievement than it was.

REFERENCES

1. *The History of the English Civil Warrs in English Verse*, 1662. Anthony (or Andrew) Cooper fought in Lord Darcy's regiment.
2. Wood I p. 68.
3. ibid. p. 70.
4. Clarendon states (VI p. 168), rather naively, it would seem, 'The affection of the University of Oxon. was most eminent . . . they now made him a new present.'
5. Wood I p. 94.
6. Bulstrode.
7. Ludlow.
8. Wood I p. 91.
9. ibid. p. 97.
10 and 11. Fasnacht/Blackwell.

Chapter Five

Discipline

'He [the Captain] ought to carry a cheerful countenance when
they do well and otherwise if they carelessly disregard
his commands he is to look upon them harshly.'

Lieutenant-Colonel Richard Elton   1659

In the view of a seventeenth-century militarist discipline
could only be achieved by exercise, order, compulsion and
example.[1] He also held that a fifth requirement was reward,
or the expectation of it, but in truth the most important is
discipline. Discipline is something that exists deep down in a
man. If it is there then the example of an Astley, a Hopton, a
Rupert will bring it to the surface, if it is not, the lash and the
gibbet cannot implant it. Exercise is necessary, for 'no man is
born a soldier, nor can attain to any excellency in that act but
by practice',[2] but given the example of a valiant commander,
order exists and compulsion is unnecessary. The Royalist
army was subject to martial law at least as early as September
1642, and in the same month Essex issued his *Lawes and
Ordinances of Warre*.[3] Since they were very similar to the
King's, it may be as well to examine them. They were very
comprehensive, listed under eleven headings, and were sub-
divided into clauses. There were 'duties moral', 'duties to
God', 'duties in camp and garrison', 'duties of victuallers',
'duties of commanding officers' and so on. The officers were as
much catered for as the men and the penalties were harsh in
the extreme. Throwing away one's weapons, abandoning the
colours, killing an enemy who had yielded, surrendering a
fort 'without the utmost necessity', carried the death penalty.
If a fortress should be lost through the officers and men

forcing the Governor to treat then 'all officers shall be punished with death and soldiers will draw lots, for one in ten shall hang'. The lesser punishments included the boring of the tongue with a hot iron for blasphemy and loss of pay for unlawful oaths, while several offences were covered by a blanket phrase strangely reminiscent of 'at the Commanding Officer's discretion' in today's 'Queen's Rules and Regulations'.

At the beginning of the war few officers indeed, on either side, were in a position to enforce discipline, for often the men got rid of officers whom, for one reason or another, they detested. Holles's regiment got their Lieutenant-Colonel, Henry Billingsley, cashiered by the simple expedient of refusing to obey him. It would seem that the whole affair was instigated by two captains, Francis and Beacon, doubtless because in the absence of the Colonel he had tried to instil some discipline in the unit. For this he was described as a 'Godamme blade and doubtlesse hatche in hell'.[4]

Until the war progressed and the civilian soldier of 1642 became the veteran of 1644, and until the officers acquired the habit of command and the men the habit of obedience, it was to be a stormy relationship. Many were the instances of plunder and pillage that were savagely punished. Prince Maurice commanded 'that one of his soldiers should be hanged, and have a ticket written on him, for plundering the Lord Robartes his house.' Although Robartes was with Essex, his house had probably been given protection because the King wanted to quarter there. At any rate he was there on 13 July 1644, and was again in Wiltshire on 16 August of the same year. 'In the middle way (between Dagleworth and Badminton) two foot soldiers were hanged on the trees in the hedgerow, for pillaging of the country villages. The whole army of horse and foot marched by the bodyes.' It was impossible to restrain the light-fingered soldiery, particularly in borderline cases. For instance Sir John Byron's men, quartered on the Parliamentarian Bulstrode Whitelocke in November 1642, possessed themselves of his horses and provender, which might be considered fair game, but also did

A grim reminder!

malicious damage to his property, which was not. Gradually,
however, the laws were implemented and the offenders made
to realise that punishment would undoubtedly follow crime,
so that some measure of discipline was established.

The system was not helped by the fact that those in command, even up to and including the King, found that they
could not always harden their hearts to carry out the extreme
penalty. On 13 January 1643, a gibbet was erected at the east
side of the conduit at Carfax in Oxford. Next day, which was
market day, at about 11 a.m., 'there was one brought thither
which should have been executed for some offence or other . . .
but was pardoned by the King and, as I heard, was only
burned in the hand and shoulder'.[5] This same gibbet seems to
have been in some demand. On 30 March

4. Fortifications at Newark, Notts. Above: West bastion looking south-east, (below) from the south-west (*Queen's Sconce, Royal Commission on Historical Monuments, England*)

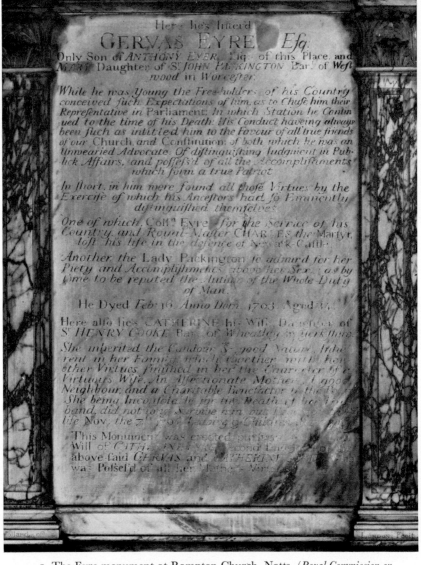

Here lies Interd
GERVAS EYRE Esq.
Only Son of ANTHONY EYRE, Esq. of this Place, and
MARY Daughter of Sr JOHN PACKINGTON Bart of West
wood in Worcester.

While he was Young the Free-holders of his Country
conceived such Expectations of him, as to Chuse him their
Representative in Parliament; In which Station he Continued to the time of his Death: His Conduct haveing always
been such as intitled him to the Favour of all true friends
of our Church and Constitution; of both which he was an
Unwearied Advocate. Of distinguishing Judgment in Pub-
lick Affairs, and possess'd of all the Accomplishments
which form a true Patriot

In short, in him were found all those Virtues by the
Exercise of which his Ancestors had so Eminently
distinguished themselves.

One of which, Coll. Eyre for the Service of his
Country, and Royal-Master CHARLES the Martyr,
lost his life in the defence of Newark-Castle.

Another the Lady Packington so admir'd for her
Piety and Accomplishments above her Sex; as by
some to be reputed the Author of the Whole Duty
of Man.

He Dyed Feb: 16 Anno Dom 1703 Aged 34.

Here also lies CATHERINE his Wife, Daughter of
Sr HENRY COOKE Bart of Wheatley in Yorkshire.

She inherited the Candour & good Nature of the
rent in her family which together with her
other Virtues finished in her the Character of a
Virtuous Wife, An Affectionate Mother, a good
Neighbour, and a Charitable Benefactor to the Poor
She being Inconsolate for the Death of her Husband, did not long Survive him but Departed this
life Nov: the 7 1704 leaving 9 Children behind her

This Monument was erected pursuant to the
Will of CATHERINE the second Daughter of the
above said GERVAS and CATHERINE who dyeing
was Possess'd of all her Father's Virtues

5. The Eyre monument at Rampton Church, Notts. (*Royal Commission on Historical Monuments, England*)

. . . three soldiers were brought to the gibbet . . . to be hanged for runninge away from their collours; but then word came from the court that but one of them three was to suffer for all the rest and that the dice should be cast to trie who that one should be: but when all came to all, other word was brought, that the Prince [of Wales] had begged all their lives and so they were pardoned all three.[6]

However, the hangman was not always frustrated: on 18 March 'a soldier hanged upon the gibbet . . . for killing a woman dwellinge about Gloster Halle or Brookenhayes etc'.[7] With all the brutality of the branding iron and the gibbet it is perhaps surprising that the lash was not as much in use as it was to be in the next century, though Symonds records one strange example: 'This day [24 May 1645], a foot soldjer was tyed (with his shoulders and breast naked) to a tree and every carter of the trayne and carriages was to have a lash; for ravishing two women. *Secundum Usum Hispaniarum*.'.

THE PROVOST

According to Thomas Venn the duties of the provost of a regiment were numerous. He had to see that all proclamations, orders and decrees issued by the provost marshal of the army were published abroad. Once a week he was to report what prisoners he had in his charge and the nature of their offences. When booty was taken it was his task to see that there was a fair and equitable division of spoil amongst the companies—a task one certainly does not envy! The camp had to be kept clean, with all garbage and filth buried. In this we can see the forerunner of the fatigue parties so familiar to any serviceman or ex-serviceman. He also controlled the victuallers, seeing that their prices were fair and that their hours of trading were within the regulations. Should he then have any spare time he was to go about the camp thrice daily to correct any wrongdoers, once in the morning, once in the afternoon and 'once in the dead of night if it can be conveniently arranged'.[9] Truly a full-time job!

QUARRELS

There seem to have existed rivalries and animosities between various foot regiments and the foot and horse generally. Wharton tells how on 4 September he was robbed by a troop of horse belonging to Colonel Foynes and lost goods to the value of £3. He would have lost his sword had he not threatened that his men would open fire on the pillagers. Then there was the glorious brawl between the captains of the blue coats (Lord Saye's regiment) and the russets (Colonel Thomas Grantham's regiment) in which their men joined, 'some of them being in drink'. They fought 'with their naked swordes',[10] some losing their thumbs and some their fingers. One such quarrel ended tragically: an officer ran his opponent through on horseback, presumably before he could retaliate, when they fell out at Cirencester on 12 July 1644. Without waiting to plead self-defence or any other mitigating circumstances, the officer, by name of Plowman, 'fled immediately', obviously believing discretion was the better part of valour.

DUELS

There is ample evidence of the existence of the 'affair of honour' at the time of the Civil War. Basically it seems to have been illegal[10] but equally certainly it seems to have gone unpunished in the main. Sir Edward Nicholas, writing to Prince Rupert on 11 May 1643, stated 'Sir James Mills was lately shot by an officer upon a private quarrel and the last night Lieutenant Cranefield (Lifeguard F) was wounded by one Captain Hastings upon a like occasion. There is here no punishment and therefore nothing but disorder may be expected.' Wood's journal leaves no doubt that these were no isolated occurrences but quite commonplace—15 March 1643, 'a duell betwixt the Lord John (Stuart), one of the Duke of Richmond's brothers, and Mr (John) Ashburnham, a gent of his majesties bedchamber, at the further end of Christ-church meadows; no hurt done on either side'[11] and so on. Although the presence of the Court at Oxford made it

A duel

likely that there were more of these affairs going on, they were by no means confined to that city. Symonds relates that at Chard on 24 July 1644, 'this morning was a duel inter the Earl of Peterborough and Captain Thomas Willoughby, whose father is steward to the Earl of Northampton; Willoughby wounded in the shoulder and thigh the Earl safe without hurt. Willoughby challenged'.

COURTS MARTIAL

The order establishing courts martial in the Parliamentarian army ran as follows:[12]

That his Excellency taking notice of the manifold abuses and injuries committed by the rude part of Soldiers to the great

damage and prejudice of the People . . . hath therefore
granted commissions, thereby enabling the Commissioners
of each regiment to sit in a council of war so often as need
may require and to punish offenders according to the laws
and ordinances of war . . . as if the offenders were tried at
Headquarters except in cases extending to Life and Limb
which are to be tried at Headquarters only.

WOODEN HORSE

Two boards were nailed together at the edges at right angles
to form a sharp ridge. This was supposed to be the backbone
of the horse and was supported at either end by two posts for
legs. Often the resemblance was completed by a rough
representation of the horse's head and tail. The offender was
made to sit on the sharp ridge for a certain period of time, the
length of which was determined by the seriousness of the
offence! His arms would be tied and often a musket or
perhaps two or three would be tied to his feet. A picture of
this beast may be found in Grose's *Military Antiquities*.[13]

THE GAUNTLET

If the crime was severe but not quite severe enough for the
maximum penalty, the running of the gauntlet was employed.
This was imported by those professionals who had seen
Swedish service. The offender was stripped to the waist and
his regiment was formed in two lines armed with cudgels. He
had to run through the lane so formed and the soldiers
belaboured him as he passed, each man getting in as many
blows as he might.

THE STRAPPADO

In this the offender was suspended by his thumbs so that his
feet just touched the ground, muskets being laid over his
shoulders, the number of which was determined by the
seriousness of the offence.

Running the gauntlet

P.B.

CAMP FOLLOWERS

Amongst the army of seamstresses, washerwomen and
drudges who catered for the material needs of the soldiers
inevitably there were those who catered for their physical
needs. It was laid down that if a whore 'was a married woman
she should be killed, but if single she should be whipped and
thrust out from the camp',[14] but, as with other laws, this one
was overlooked and seldom, if ever, was the harsher penalty
invoked. In some cases, however, particularly in the camps of
the 'Saints', they were dealt with. On 27 August 1642 at
Coventry, one of these ladies of easy virtue who had hopefully
followed the army from London was 'taken by the soldiers,
and first led about the city, then duckt in a river, then at the
last banisht from the city'. Which should have been enough to
cool her ardour! At Edgehill neither Charles nor Essex can be
said to have had an army that was under more than minimal
discipline. With death and desertion fining down the ranks,
by the time of Marston Moor they were fighting units, rather
than collections of individuals.

Spoils of war!

REFERENCES

1. Venn p. 2.
2. Bariffe p. 1.
3. Quoted in full in the Appendix.
4. Wharton.
5. Wood I p. 82.
6. ibid. p. 93.
7. ibid. p. 91.
8. Symonds's diary p. 176.
9. Venn pp. 188–9.
10. See Appendix.
11. Wood I p. 91.
12. Rushworth VII p. 816.
13. Vol. II p. 111.
14. See Appendix.

Chapter Six

Training and Ceremonial

'The soldier that expects advancement . . . must be so stout in his
resolutions as to perfectly perform what is commanded'

Captain Thomas Venn   1635

In 1642 the country had been so long at peace that few indeed
knew anything of the usages of war and veterans returning from
the continental wars were eagerly sought after, retained, well
paid and promoted by both sides. Obviously there were not
sufficient of them to go round so that, perforce, the new, raw
officer, totally ignorant of weapons and drill, faced with the
dilemma of making soldiers of the civilians he had recruited
in a short time, must have been glad to have been able to buy
a copy of Lieutenant William Bariffe's book *Military Discipline*,
which first appeared in London in 1635 and was reprinted in
1639 and again in 1643. One wonders if he blatantly walked
about with it in his hand or secretly studied it before giving
the lesson, thus keeping just one jump ahead of the men.
Another military author of the time was John Raynford,
whose book *The Young Soldier* came out in 1642. Bariffe had
very definite notions about the making of a soldier: 'By
practice is gained knowledge, knowledge begets confidence
and courage. Few or none being fearful to execute what by
frequent practice they have thoroughly acquired.' His treatise
is 374 pages long (second edition) and is very thorough, deal-
ing with pike and musket as well as other matters. Although
Captain Thomas Venn's *Military Observations* appeared in
1672, by comparison there had been very little change in
formation and drill so that it can be accepted along with
Bariffe as an authority for the Civil War.

With good reason Essex told his officers, 'They were not to

busy them [the men] in practising the more ceremonious forms of military discipline',[1] for the books, after delineating the more simple movements, go into the most complicated manoeuvres which one would imagine would baffle the most experienced troops. Some of the commands advocated by Venn must have been as tongue-twisting to the captain as they were incomprehensible to the men. Imagine shouting, 'Half double your front to the right and files double your depth to the left', or 'Bringer up stand, the rest pass through to the left and place yourself behind your bringer up.' The mind boggles at the chaos that would be caused if one tried this on inexperienced troops. Venn gets further involved when he advocates three types of countermarching—Chosean, Lacedemonian and Macedonian. The officer 'will not only find them serviceable but all delightful in private exercises'.[2] But these airy flights of fancy apart, both books contain much sound common sense and must have been invaluable to the fledgling officer keen on getting his unit into shape. Amongst the foot there was seemingly a feeling that to be a pikeman was a little more stylish than being a musketeer: 'In point of antiquity and honour the Gentlemen of the Pike craveth the precedence';[3] 'It is most proper for the Captain to exercise the pikes himself.' On 25 August 1642 Holles's regiment was told 'all the soldiers should attend their colours every morn by six of the clock to march into the field to practise, which is done accordingly'. We know just what they did so early in the day from Venn, who states that when the company had been drawn up, 'silence being commanded', the captain would start to expound to the men the 'several distances between rank and file with the ways to open and close them', and if he had sufficient patience or sanity left after an hour or two of instructing people who knew not their left hand from their right he went on to teach them the 'postures and the true using of their armes'. To make things easier for the men in the ranks he would have to make some 'special rules and observations' to help them to remember the sequence. The drill in its simple form was not difficult but one wonders if the exasperated officers ever exclaimed, as the writer has heard modern

drill sergeants do, 'You're waving those rifles [for rifle read
pike] about like a lot of pregnant butterflies!'

If at first sight the drill for the pike seems difficult, it was as
nothing compared with that of the musket. From the
shoulder to the firing and back again, Bariffe details forty
different movements. That they were criminally careless with
the musket there was little doubt. We find that Lieutenant-
Colonel Arthur Swayne was 'slain by his boy, teaching him
to use his arms. He bid the boy aim at him (thinking his gun
had not been charged) which he did only too well.' Also the
soldiers marched 'very sadly two miles' after a member of
Captain Francis's company, 'forgetting he was charged with a
bullet shot a maid through the head'[4] killing her instantly. It
might seem that any officer or NCO standing in front of a
squad teaching the rudiments of the musket deserved danger
money. Both books are nothing if not comprehensive, Venn
going so far as to include movements for both the snaphance
and matchlock muskets. The instrument designed to make all
their movements harmonious was the drum, which was 'the
voice of the Commander, the spur of the valiant and the heart
of the coward'. It was by the drum, not the bugle, that orders
were given to the foot, 'when the roaring cannon, the clash of
arms and other confused noise causeth that neither Captain
nor other officers can be heard'. Every man had to recognise
six different beats and to interpret their meaning correctly:[5]

1. *A Call:*   By a call you must understand to hear your
                present engagements [orders].
2. *A Troop:*   Shoulder your muskets, advance pikes, close
                ranks and troop along [follow] your officer
                to the rendezvous.
3. *A March:*   By this you understand to take open order in
                rank. Shoulder muskets and pikes. To direct
                your march quicker or slower according to
                the beat.
4. *Preparative:* Close to due distance for skirmish in rank
                and file, to make ready that you may
                execute on first command.

5. *A Battle:*   Battle or Charge. Pressing forward in order of battle, without lagging behind, rather boldly stepping forward into the place of him who drops dead or wounded before thee.

6. *A Retreat:*   Understand an orderly withdrawal backward for advantage of ground or other politic reason, to draw the enemy into some ambushment or the like.

Then came the great day when the company had no choice but to march out, whether trained well or ill. The captain led the van composed of eight ranks of musketeers four deep. The first drummer was in the midst of these. Then followed eight ranks of pikemen led by the ensign (who bore the colour) and also the second drummer. A sergeant headed another contingent of pikemen of the same strength (with another drum), while the rear was brought up by another eight ranks of musketeers under the senior sergeant with the fourth drummer. The last man, who marched behind the company, was the lieutenant. From this point of vantage he could check on the alignment of the ranks and, more important, stop the men straggling or deserting.

BASIC PIKE DRILL AND COMMANDS (after Bariffe)

Stand to your arms: The men carrying their pikes form up on a marker. They adopt an attitude feet apart about 9 inches. The pike grasped easily by the right hand, the butt about 12 inches from the right foot. The left hand rests on the hip.

Have a care: A cautionary command similar to the modern 'Attention'.

Advance your Pikes: 1. The right hand raises the pike to the extremity of its reach. The left hand grasps the pike at waist level.

2. The right hand supports the base of the pike. The left hand returns to the hip.

The pike should now be securely and comfortably resting on the right shoulder in an upright position.

The men are now in a position preparatory to marching off. Should the officer wish to march them off he would command: To your left hand [or right hand] face, then: To your front march.

Most of the other postures were assumed from the advance. They were:

Charge your Pike: For use when advancing against an enemy.

1. The pike comes forward into a horizontal position, supported by the left hand at its full extent while the right hand, still on the butt, is in the vicinity of the cheek. To support this movement comfortably the left foot is advanced half a pace.

2. The pike is now brought back to the full extent of the right arm while the left is close to the body. The left foot is returned so that its heel rests against the instep of the right foot. This was also used in giving a general salute.

Charge to Horse: The position assumed for receiving a cavalry charge. This was taken up from the close order position, that is, similar to the posture adopted for 'Stand to your arms' but with the pike placed on the inside of the right foot.

1. The left leg moves forward a full pace, with the knee bent and the

right leg extended. The butt of the pike rests against the instep of the right foot.

2. The left hand grasps the pike with the left elbow resting on the left knee. The position should be quite comfortable and capable of being maintained without discomfort. The right hand now draws the sword over the top of the left arm and it is held ready with the point resting on the ground to avoid fatigue.

These are the basic postures but others may be mentioned in passing:

Assume a Lazy Posture:	Equivalent to the modern 'Stand at ease'.
Cheek your Pikes:	A sentinel posture.
Trail your Pikes:	Seldom used, but when, for example, troops moved by night or through a wood, the file leader grasped his pike by the head and the second man grasped it by the butt and so on down the line, so that no one got lost. Also used in a funeral procession, the seventeenth-century equivalent of the modern 'Reverse your arms'.
Comport your Pikes:	Useful when going uphill.
Port your Pikes:	Invented for the rear files when the front files are charged.

BASIC MUSKET DRILL AND COMMANDS (after Bariffe)

As has been already stated the musket loading and firing drill is too lengthy to examine here but the basic postures for parade or marching were these:

The same order that brought the pikeman on parade sufficed

for the musketeers although it seems that if musketeers alone were to be on parade the command might be *Form a body*. The primary position was with the feet apart, the rest in the left hand, the butt by the toe of the shoe while the musket was in the right hand with the butt similarly by the toe of the right shoe.

Have a Care:	The right hand is brought up the musket barrel to chest level. The left hand slides up the rest until the left hand is able to hook itself over the fork of the rest.
Shoulder your Musket:	1. The right hand descends the musket to its full reach and raises it. The rest is similarly raised by the left hand. Bring the two together in line with the chin.
	2. The left hand carries the musket on to the shoulder, gripping the butt. The right hand brings the rest down to the right foot.

During the march the rest is used in the elegant out-and-in motion generally associated with the Georgian dandies.

Fire your piece!

GUN DRILL

What Bariffe, Elton, Markham and Raynford did for the foot William Eldred did for the gunner. His *Gunners Glasse*, published in 1646, runs to 107 pages and is a remarkable document for all those interested in the artillery of the period. It sets out in the form of a dialogue between 'gunner' and 'scholar' all the intricacies of the artilleryman's art, with very many hints and tips of a practical nature.

The drill given by Eldred was as follows:

Put back your Piece: This meant returning the cannon to its original position because in those days, before hydraulic dampening, the shock of the recoil would drive the piece backwards.

Order your Piece to Load: Remove the elevating wedge and depress the breach so that the muzzle was raised ready for loading.

Search your Piece: The barrel was scoured to remove any remains from the last round.

Sponge your Piece: A continuation of the last order when the barrel was sponged and dried to make sure there was no smouldering debris which might cause a premature explosion.

Fill your Ladle: The issue powder for each piece was stored in a 'budge barrel' kept at the rear of the gun in action. Between each discharge it was the duty of a member of the crew to cover the top to prevent accidental discharge. Such accidents, through negligence, were not uncommon. The ladle mentioned in the order was of a particular size to contain the correct amount of powder for the type of gun employed, and would be filled at the barrel and returned.

Put in your Powder and *Empty your ladle*	were the next two orders and are self-explanatory.
Put home your Powder:	A rammer was used to compress the powder in the breach.
Thrust home your Wad:	Wadding was rammed down on the powder to keep it in place and also to seal in the explosive gases.
Regard your Shot:	The gunner would inspect the ball for size and imperfections which, if found, he would endeavour to make allowances for in his calculations.
Put home your Shot gently:	Again self-explanatory.
Thrust home your last Wad in three Strokes:	The last wad was placed to keep the projectile in place, very necessary if the gun was at a low elevation.
Gauge your Piece:	By this was meant the laying of the gun onto the target.

The piece was now ready for firing, which was accomplished either by a fuse or a piece of match attached to a long staff.

CAVALRY

John Cruso catered for the training needs of the Cavalry in his manual *Instructions for the Cavall'rie, rectified and supplied according to the present practice of the Low Country Warres*, published in 1623.[6] Perhaps the most surprising thing about these training manuals of the seventeenth century is the thoroughness of the authors. Very little is generalised or skimped. Cruso divides his work into four parts and, in the fantastic number of sixty chapters, covers every aspect of cavalry work, which must have made it a necessity for every novice officer to have the book in his saddle-bag.

COMPLIMENTS

Whilst on the march it was sometimes necessary to give compliments to friends or superiors and it could have been the

6. Prince Rupert of the Rhine. A portrait by Gerard von Honthorst
(*Städtische Galerie, Landesmuseum, Hanover*)

7. A Royalist officer, Colonel Sir Francis Gamul, pictured in the stained-glass window in the Barnston Chapel, Farndon, Cheshire (*Photograph: E. Preston*)

company we have followed through their training, fairly
efficient but still rather trigger happy, that Fanshawe talks
about when he relates:

> We, all my household being present, heard drums beat in
> the highway, over the garden wall. My father asked me if I
> would go upon the mount to see the soldiers march, for it
> was Sir Charles Lee's company of foot, an acquaintance of
> ours. I said yes and went up leaving my back to a tree that
> grew on the mount. The commander, seeing us there, in
> compliment gave us a volley of shot, and one of their
> muskets being loaded, shot a brace of bullets not two inches
> above my head as I leaned to the tree . . .

The post of ensign was not easily filled. His place was 'to
express all the Gallantry he can . . . either in displaying his
colours standing, marching, charging and retreating'.[7]
Besides being a stout warrior, for 'a greater act of cowardice
cannot be found than to suffer the colours to be lost', he had
to be quick-witted and athletic like John Gwyn at First
Newbury. Bearing the colour of Salusbury's regiment he
'jumped over hedge and ditch, or I had died by a multitude
of hands',[8] when the Parliamentarian horse forced the
regiment to retreat. But the ensign had to be far more than
this. To him fell the main duty of paying compliments and
Venn details eleven postures, as complicated as the foot
commands mentioned earlier. For instance: 'With turns or
flourishes you bring the butt end of the staff to your left hand
turning the palm of the left hand outward . . . and with the
same hand only throw it off upon its turn with a flourish to
deliver it into the left hand and to perform the same with the
left hand and deliver the colours as at first into the right
hand.' To give compliments to the general or any noble
stranger, 'the Ensign bearer in all humility is to bow the head
of his colours waving them with the bow of his body and to
raise both it and himself up again and as the said person shall
pass away the drum shall beat and the colours shall be
displayed'.

Paying compliments

CEREMONIAL

Once again the ensign was at the centre of things. For the
lodging of the colour, for instance, a body of pikemen were to
stand in the rear, with the ensign at the head. The captain
was to proceed before the colours with the drums and
sergeants on each side of them with the lieutenant to the
rear. 'Then shall they troop up with the colours furled to . . .
their quarters . . . he [the ensign] shall with a bow to the
Captain carry in his colours. The musketeers will make ready,
that being done they shall all present, and upon the beat of
drum or other word of command give one entire volley. Then
command every officer to go to his quarters.'[9] And the same
for the entering of a town: '. . . then he shall unfold or open
his colours and let them fly at full length . . . this is a marching
in triumph; but if the wind blow stiff . . . then he may set the
butt against his waist but not otherwise and is to have but
one hand upon his staff in any march whatever.'

As in the case of the legionary standard the colours were to be regarded as semi-sacred. The ensign must never lay his colours on the ground 'or put them in unworthy hands', but must fold them and maintain them in an upright position with the sergeants' halberds and he was not to 'go from the sight of them unless he shall leave a sufficient guard for them'. For a funeral procession we find an illustration in that of George Stuart, Lord d'Aubigny, captain of the Duke of York's troop, who was mortally wounded at Edgehill on 23 October 1642. His 'great solemn funeral'[10] took place in Oxford nearly three months later:

> The body was brought up from Magdalen College and so brought and attended all the way through the street to Christ Church the Cathedral and there entered. The foot-men soldiers came first with their muskets under their arms, the noses of the muskets being behind them. The pikemen trailed their pikes on the ground, the horsemen followed with their pistols in their hands the handles being upward, the tops of the auntients [standards] also was borne behind. A chariot covered with black velvet where the body was drawn by six horses etc. The man that drove the chariot strewed money about the street as he passed. Three great volleys of shot at the entering of the body and lastly a herald of arms proclaimed his titles.

WAR MUSIC

I had intended to head this section 'Martial Music', but it has been pointed out to me by Lewis Winstock,[11] who has done much pioneering work in researching Civil War music, that this is simply music scored for military bands, and that 'War Music' is a blanket term covering the whole field of music used by soldiers during hostilities. Not only marches but songs of a martial or sentimental nature are included. He states that the only criterion is really whether they were popular with, and used by, the soldiery.

Adopting this as a yardstick one can probe amongst such

fragments as are left to us in journals, letters and accounts. All through history there is proof that men's spirits are elevated by the sound of their own, or other people's voices. This is probably why the ancient Spartans found that the lame singer Tyrtaeus was one of their most successful generals. The Norman minstrel Taillefer led the first charge against the Saxon line on Caldbec Hill chanting the *Song of Roland* while his supporting knights roared out the chorus 'Aoi!' All too often, however, we find that the words survive and the tune does not, or vice versa. One might give much to learn the words of a song employed by John Gwyn who, incensed that a party of Waller's horse had beaten up the quarters at Devizes and got away scot-free, determined to retaliate. Taking a party of his friends, 'twenty-seven officers and reformadoes', he travelled 10 miles over the downs to attack Waller's rearguard at Marlborough town end.[12] 'Withal strictly resolved, that not a word should be spoken after once their swords were drawn . . . but to unanimously sing "a brisk, lively tune, and so to fall on singing as they did", beat the enemy, pursuing them through the town at midday.' The music survived – the words did not.

Other ballads, however, survived intact and seem to have been as popular in their day as 'Roll out the barrel' and 'We'll hang out the washing on the Siegfried line' were in the Second World War. A sample with a gay, catchy tune and verses almost complete is given at the end of this chapter.

At the camp fire or on the march we can imagine the Royalists singing many songs of a sentimental, bawdy or humorous nature, with airs and words that we find acceptable and memorable even to our rather more sophisticated tastes. My favourite is, without doubt, a rollicking drinking song that goes 'Of all the brave birds that ever I see, The owl is the fairest in her degree . . . '. The idea, fathered in Victorian times, that the Roundheads were sober, canting and austere to a man is, of course, as faulty as most generalities. Even Cromwell himself drank wine upon occasion, loved good music and permitted dancing at his daughter Bridget's wedding; while a Cambridge don complained that the

Parliamentarian troops billeted in the colleges wanted 'fiddlers and revels day and night'.[13]

Still using our term 'War Music' in its fullest sense we must include the psalms and hymns used by the Roundheads: there is nothing like the imminent possibility of violent death to turn soldiers' thoughts to higher things. In 1643 Lord Brook's men chanted the 149th psalm as they stormed Lichfield Close: 'Let the high praises of God be in their mouths and a two-edged sword in their hand', and, most appropriately, 'To bind their kings with chains and their nobles with links of iron'.[14] After Dunbar, Cromwell halted his Ironsides, probably to blow their horses, and bade them sing Psalm 117, 'Praise the Lord all ye nations, praise him all ye people, for his merciful kindness is great towards us and the truth of the Lord endureth for ever'. These 'holy exercises' came to be considered typical of the Parliamentarian army; they sang in the cornfields of Marston Moor, they sang in the streets of Preston, at Second Newbury and at Winceby. John Vicars exults, 'They [the enemy] only knew them to be Parliament soldiers by their singing of psalms, a blessed badge and cognisance indeed.'[15]

Much use was made of musical instruments—the trumpet, the drum, and to a lesser degree the fife and violin. Of course, when the Scots became allied with Parliament, the pipes assumed some prominence. So many instances of their use occur in Civil War literature that an entire volume could be written on them.

WHEN CANNONS ARE ROARING

Soldiers with Swords in hands
To the walls coming
Horsemen about the streets
Riding and running
Sentinels on the walls
Arm, arm, a-crying
Petards against the ports
Wild fire a-flying.

When cannons are roaring
And bullets are flying

He that would honour win
Must not fear dying.

Trumpets on turrets high
    These are a-sounding
Drums beating out aloud
    Echoes resounding
Alarm bells in each place
    They are a-ringing
Women with stones in lap
    To the walls bringing.

When cannons are roaring etc.

Captains in open fields
    On their foes rushing
Gentlemen second them
    With their pikes pushing
Engineers in the trench
    Earth, earth, uprearing
Gunpowder in the Mines
    Pagans up blowing.

When cannons are roaring etc.

Portcullis in the ports
    They are down letting
Burgers come flocking by
    Too their hands setting
Ladders against the walls
    They are uprearing
Women great timber logs
    To the walls bearing.

When cannons are roaring etc.

(John Forbes, *Cantos, Songs and Fancies*, 1662)

REFERENCES

1. Davies p. 35.
2. Venn p. 108.
3. ibid. p. 34.
4. Wharton.

5. Bariffe p. 12.
6. Now reprinted by Roundwood Press.
7. Venn p. 185.
8. Atkyns/Gwyn p. 53.
9. Venn.
10. Wood.
11. See Bibliography.
12. Atkyns/Gwyn p. 64.
13. Barwick, *Querela Cantabrigiensis* p. 15.
14. Gresley, *Siege of Lichfield* p. 66.
15. John Vicars (the Roundhead pamphleteer), *Jehovah Jireh* III
    p. 281.

Chapter Seven

Food and Drink

Some hae meat, and canna eat,
    And some wad eat that want it;
But we hae meat and we can eat,
    And sae the Lord be thank it.

Robert Burns

To understand the diet of the seventeenth century one must first appreciate the environment of the time. Between 1600 and 1688 the purchase of land doubled as speculators who had invested profitably in great trading ventures such as the East India Company poured their profits into the purchase and development of great estates. They also expected these to yield a profit, experimenting with new crops and methods of husbandry, to the eventual benefit of everyone. Many more acres were put under the plough and many books on agriculture and gardening appeared. The vegetable garden came into greater prominence and more fruit and vegetables became available.

This new prosperity, however, was a long while percolating down to the poorer classes, whose lot was not enviable. John Evelyn comments in his diary: 'Most of the rural parishes are but of mud and the people living as wretchedly as in the most impoverished parts of France.' The state of the harvest had a great effect on the economies of all, but particularly upon the poorer classes who were little able to cope with the often sharp fluctuations in the price of bread. The four commodities on which the poor or labouring classes seem to have based their economy were cheese, beer, beef and bread. In times of high prices meat might disappear altogether from their table and broth, made with peas and beans, take its place. The country-man could supplement this diet with rabbits or birds poached from his landlord and with scanty vegetables from his own garden, but the townsman had no such opportunities. Sheep's heads and pig's trotters supplemented his unappetising fare of salt fish and cheese, but as usual, these shortcomings passed over the heads of the rich and middle classes, who ate a great deal of meat, especially at dinner. Pepys tells us that on 4 April 1663, when he gave a dinner, there was 'fricassee of rabbits and chicken, a leg of mutton boiled, three carps in a dish, a great dish of a side of lamb, a dish of roasted pigeons, a dish of four lobsters, three tarts, a lamprey pie, a most rare pie, a dish of anchovies, good wine of all sorts and all things mighty noble.' One wonders if the company all retired to sleep it off! Breakfast was eaten early. Our ancestors would have been offended by the suggestion of a continental break-fast – they sat down to a variety of cold meats, cheese, fish and ale. Supper was a more moderate meal.

So however frugal the common soldier's daily ration of two pounds of bread, one pound of meat (or an equal amount of cheese) and one bottle of wine (or two of beer) may seem to us, it may not have represented any particular hardship to him. This issue bread was two-thirds wheat and one-third rye with an admixture of bran and meal. Before Edgehill the army hardly had time to get organised and on both sides the common soldier seems to have gone hungry. Clarendon asserts that there were 'very many companies of the common soldier who had scarce eaten bread in eight and forty hours',[1] while Ludlow tells us somewhat ruefully that when he did eventually obtain food, he could scarcely eat it, 'my jaws for want of use almost lost their natural faculty'.[2]

Once the Royalists got organised, however, they endeav-oured to provide for their men methodically. From the head-quarters at Oxford bread was baked regularly under the supervision of the Waggon Master General and issued as required, but the scale of rations as laid down could not be adhered to. Often bread and water were substituted. In unusual circumstances even drinking water was scarce. After

Marston Moor, Lord Manchester's troops 'drained the wells to the mud, were necessitated to drink water out of ditches and out of places puddled with horses' feet . . . very few of the common soldiers did eat above the quantity of a penny loaf from Tuesday to the Saturday morning and had no beer at all',[3] owing to the complete breakdown of their supply system. Manchester told them that 'although he could not possibly that night make provision for them . . . yet he would without fail endeavour their satisfaction in the morning.' The officers obviously did not share this common fare but would supply themselves with a more varied diet from their sumpter (pack-horse); and the richer ones would have brought their body servants with them so that they would suffer the minimum of inconvenience.

Of course, the army could not have been held together if this state of affairs had prevailed all the time. There were times of plenty – when the Parliamentarians surprised Cirencester on 16 September 1643 they found thirty cartloads of victuals provided by the Royalist commissaries for their own men. Meat was preserved by salting, drying and pickling which, we may be sure, did not improve the flavour at all and probably needed plenty of beer to wash it down. According to Robert Boyle, there were experiments to improve the taste and keeping power of meat. Aboard ship it was roasted, cut into small pieces and packed in a barrel. The whole was then sealed by filling the spaces with melted butter. It kept for over six months in this manner without taint. Ideally, an army always kept a herd of animals with it, 'meat on the hoof' so to speak. Sir James Turner, speaking of the duties of a commissary, says there should be 'as many living oxen, cows, swine, sheep, hens and turkeys as may be conveniently fed'. There could have been no shortage of people with a knowledge of butchery in the ranks, for most farm labourers kept their own pig or cow which they fattened up for meat. The battle plan of Naseby shows a big cooking pot suspended over a fire, and perhaps it is not too fanciful to suggest that after the issue of rations a number of small groups might pool their meat, boiling a stew in such a pot and supplementing the

Time out of war

meat by the addition of vegetables such as turnips, carrots and leeks, filched from the adjoining fields or gardens.

PAY

We have seen the difficulty of both arming and feeding the opposing armies. The third, and possibly the most arduous, task was paying them regularly. There was no standard rate of pay, but in December 1642 the Royalists were offering 6 shillings weekly to musketeers, 12s 10d to dragooners and 17s 10d to troopers. It was expected that they would provide their own arms and equipment. As the war wore on both armies were frequently in arrears. By 1644, the pay of the common soldier was 4 shillings weekly and Symonds tells us the pay of the other individuals was as follows:[4]

	£	s	d
Captain	2	12	6
Lieutenant	1	8	0
Ensign	1	1	0
Gentleman of the Arms		10	6
Sergeants		10	6
Corporals		7	0
Drummers		7	0

Lack of pay was one of the prime reasons for desertion. Lord Fairfax wrote of this difficulty to Parliament on 12 August: 'I encounter these difficulties, first the reluctance of men to engage in other activities during harvest time; next the extreme want of money and clothes for the supply of this small army I have, which discourages others from entering in the Service and drives some of my own men to seek better wages in the harvest field.' This problem was still galling him on 20 September, for he wrote again on the subject: '. . . their stock of patience being at length worn out, our troops are ready to disband, as some of them have done already. . . . In a few days they will moulder to nothing.' Parliament did at least have the taxation of London to fall back on, but the King was soon in straitened circumstances. In January 1644 Sir

John Mennes wrote to Prince Rupert, 'Money is a thing not spoken of', and later, on 10 February, speaking of the Irish troops just disembarked, he said: 'I shall endeavour here to make what shift I can to assist them, which must be in providing victuals – for money is a thing we hear not of. . . . '

FREE QUARTER

When money was not available, the troops on both sides lived off the country, that is to say they were billeted and their hosts received tickets which were to be redeemed at the first opportunity. At Shrewsbury early in 1644, Rupert actually managed to accomplish this, which strangely did not please the men; apparently they regarded the system as a licence to plunder. Free quarter inevitably led to a slackening of discipline with increased opportunity for marauding, which no commander could tolerate. Nevertheless it is difficult to see how this could be avoided if the soldiers were not regularly paid. As early as 27 November 1642, the King gave orders to Prince Rupert authorising him to order his colonels of horse and dragoons to

> quarter and billet their respective regiments in such places as we have assigned and there to take up such necessary provision of diet, lodging, hay, oats and straw as may be necessary for them. And if there should not be sufficient for such their supply in their quarters, then they are to send out their warrants to the several hundreds and parishes adjacent, requiring the inhabitants to bring in all fitting provisions for their daily supply.[5]

With the bad harvests of the period 1630–7 and later from 1646–51, the farmers could have been in no position to offer extended help of this kind, and it is easy to see how a regiment of horse could soon wear out its welcome, even in a Royalist area.

REFERENCES

1. Clarendon I p. 83.
2. See Bibliography.
3. Firth p. 217.
4. Unpublished notebook, B M Harleian MS 986, f.96.
5. Warburton II p. 70.

Chapter Eight

Some Notable Characters

'So I took the chief of your tribes, wise men, and known, and
made them heads over you, captains over
thousands and captains over hundreds . . . '

Deuteronomy 1:15

To many people the citizens of the seventeenth century (or,
indeed, any historical period) are as remote from the people
they meet on the 8.15 every morning as *Australopithecus* or
Neanderthal man. They see them as a different species who
went about in peculiar clothes, eating meat and drinking beer
in vast quantities, but never, by any stretch of the imagination, as ordinary people with much the same ambitions, woes,
joys and failings as we have ourselves. Yet even a brief acquaintance with their diaries, letters and memoirs is sufficient
to verify that they were. To read, for instance, the journal
of Anthony Wood, a schoolboy at the time, or Lieutenant
Elias Archer's account of his campaign, is to find so many
points of similarity with our own outlook that the reader
feels himself warming towards them, laughing with them
at their follies and appreciating their moments of triumph,
however trifling. There were as great a number of
fools, saints, heroes, villains and plain ordinary folk then as
now, and it is the purpose of this chapter to delineate some of
them.

Prince Rupert

So much glamour and legend has been woven about this
dashing soldier that it is hard to determine how much is fact,

how much fiction. Clarendon describes him as being 'rough and passionate . . . [he] loved not debate, and liked what was proposed as he liked the persons that proposed it'.[1] He had learnt his soldiering during the Thirty Years War, when he had been a prisoner of war for three years. No doubt this had soured a nature that might previously have been affectionate and gracious. Certainly only his intimates, his brother Maurice, his uncle the King and his constant friend Colonel Will Legge saw this softer side of him during the Civil War.

He was tall, powerful, dressed colourfully and was abstemious in an age of hard drinkers. His reputation was made as a cavalry officer and it is in this guise that he is most often thought of. But he was much more than this: military engineering, siege work and seamanship all came within the scope of his inquiring mind. His dashing cavalry and their whirlwind charges carried all before them until the battle of Marston Moor when they were defeated by Cromwell and his Ironsides. His surrender of Bristol to Fairfax in September 1645 brought him into disrepute with the King, who exiled him. He commanded a small Royalist fleet in the Second Civil War in 1648. Returning to England at the Restoration he was instrumental in founding the Hudson Bay Company. He died in November 1682, and was buried in Westminster Abbey.

Prince Maurice, Rupert's dearly loved brother, has always been eclipsed by Rupert's brilliance, and in truth is little known to any but the student of the period. Although Clarendon speaks slightingly of him, condemning him 'being used to the company of ordinary and inferior men . . . whom he loved',[2] which caused the status-conscious historian to resent the fact that 'toward men of the best condition, with whom he might well have justified a familiarity, he maintained the full state of his birth', it is very possible that he was more generally popular than Rupert and 'fought very stoutly when there was occasion'. Going into exile with his brother he also emulated him in going to sea, and was drowned in 1652 when *The Defiance* sank with all hands.

8. Two Royalist officers. Left: Colonel John Russell. Right: Sir John Byron (*Portrait by William Dobson, reproduced by permission of Lieutenant-Colonel J. L. B. Leicester-Warren*)

9. James Graham, Marquis of Montrose (*engraving from a portrait by Van Dyck*)

Sir Thomas Glemham could be termed the most gallant but persistent loser on the Royalist side. As Governor of York, it fell to his lot to surrender the city after the disastrous battle of Marston Moor. He raised 3,000 men for the defence of Carlisle, in which he was unsuccessful. Overlooked by the King for a barony, it was his destiny always to be beaten: he was appointed Governor of Oxford when that city's fate was already sealed.

John, first Baron Byron had seen military service in the Low Countries and against the Scots prior to the Civil War. At the outbreak of hostilities he joined Rupert at Worcester and fought at Powick Bridge. At Edgehill he commanded a cavalry reserve and was prominent at the first battle of Newbury, 20 September 1643. He was elevated to be Field Marshal for north Wales and Baron Rochdale on 24 October. He commanded the right wing at Marston Moor and was notable for his stubborn defence of Chester, of which city he was Governor.

Sir Arthur Aston. An officer who apparently did not improve upon acquaintance. He is described as 'having the good fortune to be very much esteemed where he was not known and very much detested where he was'.[3] Sergeant-Major-General of Dragoons, Governor of Reading and then of Oxford (August 1643 until Christmas Day 1644), he was a proud and obstinate man. We are told that he 'purely hated' Colonel Henry Gage (of whom more later) because 'the lords had a singular esteem [of Gage] and consulted frequently with him, whilst they looked to be besieged and thought Oxford to be more secure for his being in it'.[4] Naturally this did not make the Governor feel very amicable toward Gage so that 'he crossed him in anything he proposed', and when the Marchioness of Winchester came to Oxford to solicit help for her husband, besieged in Basing House, Aston 'all too reasonably opposed the design as full of more difficulties and liable to greater damages than any soldier who understood command would expose himself . . . to'. When Gage successfully undertook this mission, the Governor's wrath and envy can be imagined. So unpopular was Aston that after being in office only four months he was attacked in the street in the dark and wounded in the side. 'The King well understood and was the more troubled because he saw the prejudice was universal and with too much reason.' He was removed from office by an unfortunate accident on 19 September 1644. He was showing off his horse's paces to impress the ladies in Bullington Green when his horse threw him, and his leg was broken so badly that it had to be amputated on 7 December. Aston was found to be unfit for further employment and given a pension of £1,000 a year. Wood tells how 'Colonel [Will] Legge succeeded him. Soon the country people coming to the market would be ever and anon asking the sentinel, "Who is Governor of Oxford?" They answered, "One Legge." Then replied they, "A pox on him! Is he Governor still?" '5 This story is probably only a boys' jest, for as Clarendon tells us Gage succeeded Aston as Governor, but it does serve to show how thoroughly detested he was. Aston met with a particularly unpleasant fate. When Drogheda was stormed by Cromwell it is said that his brains were dashed out with his own wooden leg.

Lord George Goring. He was an engaging ruffian who could 'charm birds out of a tree', as the saying goes. He had 'wit, courage, understanding and ambition uncontrolled by fear of God or man'.6 Of all his attributes, 'dissimulation was his masterpiece; in which he so excelled, that men were not ordinarily ashamed, or out of countenance, with being deceived by him but twice.' So adept was he at deception that at the beginning of the Civil War, when he was Governor of Portsmouth, he was receiving money from both the Queen and the Parliament, both being well assured that he would declare for them. The Parliament, receiving disquieting news from their agents that he was in reality a Royalist, sent for him to demand an explanation and in actual fact to imprison him if necessary. Declaring himself 'unskilled and unfit to speak before so wise and judicious an assembly',7 he played on the feelings of the House to such good effect that, not without some little apology for troubling him,

> ... they paid him a good sum of money for their arrears and shortly after he received their commission as Lieutenant-General of the Horse. Eventually, having played the Parliament for as much as he could get, he sent them a letter saying that his council had advised him that Parliament did many things illegal ... that he had been given his command of that garrison by the King, and that he durst not be absent from it, without his leave.

The mask was off and for the rest of the war he was to be Royalist. On the credit side, however, as a commander he was popular, possessing 'a keener courage and presentness of mind in danger'. His ability as a cavalry commander was amply demonstrated at Marston Moor and at Second Newbury where his charge baffled the Ironsides. Escaping from England in 1646 when the King's cause was collapsing, he finished his life in a Spanish monastery.

Sir Jacob Astley (created Baron in 1644) was a man's man and generally esteemed. A plain straightforward officer, 'in council he used few but pertinent words and was not at all pleased with the long speeches made there ... he forbore not to speak his own mind'.[8] He had great experience of the Dutch service and was Sergeant-Major-General of the Foot from 1642 to 1645. Clarendon described him as 'fit for the office he exercised ... as Christendom yielded and was so generally esteemed'. Not the least valuable of his attributes was his ability to work amicably with the Prince Palatine Rupert, whose lack of tact antagonised so many. When preparing to advance at Edgehill his men asked him to make a prayer for them. Impatient for action but knowing that they needed spiritual comfort in the face of death his reply was a masterpiece of brevity: 'O Lord! Thou knowest how busy I must be this day. If I forget thee do not thou forget me – march on boys!'

Having fought throughout the war with distinction he was one of the King's few remaining commanders in the dark days

S·B·

Your Majesty's humble servants!

of 1646. With the capable Charles Lucas he raised 2,000
infantry in Wales and came to Worcester before going to the
King's aid at Oxford. The journey was fraught with peril,
however, for there were Roundhead forces at Warwick,
Evesham and Gloucester. Despite this he managed to cross
the Avon without casualties. Colonel Morgan, the local
Parliamentary commander, sent out for cavalry and, to
hinder Astley until they arrived, skirmished on his flanks.
About 9 p.m. on the evening of 20 March, the cavalry under
Sir William Brereton arrived. Astley, cornered, took up a
defensive position on the flank of a hill near Stow-on-the-
Wold. At dawn the next day Morgan and Brereton attacked.
The Welshmen, untrained and unused to war, put up little
resistance. Sixteen hundred surrendered with their arms and
ammunition. Astley was unhorsed and surrendered. His
words were typically to the point. 'You have done your work
well, boys. You may go play, unless you fall out amongst
yourselves.'

Sir Ralph Hopton (created Baron 1643) was an independent commander known chiefly for his successes in the West Country where he upheld the King's cause in concert with Sir John Berkeley. His high position was shown in the superscription of a warrant of 21 November 1643, 'Ralph Lord Hopton, Baron of Stratton, Field Marshal of all His Majesty's western forces. . . '. He had one of the best records of victories in the Royalist cause – Braddock Down, Stratton and Lansdowne. He was 'a man superior to all temptation . . . he had a good understanding, a clear courage, an industry not to be exhausted, a virtue that none of the others had. . . . There was only one man in the council of whom nobody spoke ill . . . and that was the Lord Hopton'. But on the debit side he was 'longer in resolving and more apt to change his mind, after he had resolved, than is agreeable to the office of Commander-in-Chief'. One of the most endearing qualities of Hopton was his enduring friendship with the Roundhead general, Sir William Waller, which continued through the conflict. When Hopton suggested a meeting early in the war, Waller, fearing that it was for the purpose of seducing him from his allegiance to Parliament, wrote to him: 'Certainly my affections to you are so unchangeable, that hostility itself cannot violate my friendship to your person; but I must hold true to the cause I serve . . . I would most gladly wait upon you according to your desire but I look upon you as engaged with that party beyond all possibility of a retreat . . . Let us do it [their duty] in a way of honour and without personal animosities, whatsoever the issue may be.'[9] They were both fortunate that they were able to keep their personal feelings completely separate from their professional duties, for they lost no opportunity to outwit and out-general each other. After Waller had surprised and eliminated Colonel Richard Bolle's regiment at Alton, Hopton wrote, 'This is the first evident ill success I have had. I must acknowledge that I have lost many brave and gallant men. . . . ' He bore the loss of this regiment 'with extraordinary trouble of mind, and as a wound that would bleed inward',[10] while Waller smarted from the defeats inflicted on him by Hopton at Lansdowne and Roundway Down early in 1643.

Both were 'inflamed with desire of a battle . . . to make even all accounts'. The result was the battle of Cheriton, which was a crushing defeat for the Royalists and one of the turning-points of the war.

On 15 January 1646 Hopton was called upon to take command of 'the dissolute, undisciplined, wicked beaten army in the west'[11] and make a last ditch stand. He fortified himself in Torrington. On 16 February, Fairfax attacked and took the town. The Parliamentarian advance was delayed when the Royalist arsenal, consisting of eighty-four barrels of gunpowder situated in the church, was blown up by accident. With his now mutinous army Hopton fell back on Truro, and for a few more days held them loyal by the sheer force of his personality. But it was all to no purpose. His men refused to fight and on 9 March he opened negotiations with Fairfax. On 13 March 1646 Hopton agreed to disband his forces and go abroad. There the war ended for him.

Sir John Urry, a Scottish professional soldier, was a man of little principle. He changed sides three times in all during the war, and strangely enough was taken at his face value each time. One would have thought that he would have been executed as a traitor after the first time, but his luck did not run out until 1650, when he was executed with Montrose. A veteran of the Thirty Years War, he made himself useful to Rupert at the time of the Chalgrove Raid and, through his interest, became Major-General.

It was not only the nobility and professionals who made their mark in the Royalist cause. Three London craftsmen downed tools when they heard the call of duty and joined the colours. All three were to be immortalised, both as engravers and as soldiers. Their names were *Robert Peake, William Faithorne* and *Wenceslaus Hollar*. Peake had a shop near Holborn Bridge in London and, as his enemies were sneeringly to assert, was a 'seller of picture babies'. But he must have been a man of some standing in his community for when he joined the musketeer regiment of Sir Marmaduke Rawdon, a prosperous merchant and ship owner, he became its lieutenant-colonel. The regiment was stationed at Oxford when the Marquis of Winchester came to request the King to put a garrison into his country seat at Basing. In circumstances related later (Chapter 12), Peake led half the regiment to Basing to be followed later by the aged Rawdon with the remainder. Here he remained in the capacity of lieutenant governor until the House was taken by storm in November 1645, rendering such good service that he was knighted in Oxford on 27 March 1645. Taken prisoner, he was removed to London and imprisoned. After a while he was released and went back to his trade, eventually being succeeded by his younger brother. He died in July 1667 and was buried with military honours in St Sepulchre's Church, Holborn.

Faithorne was apprenticed to Peake for two or three years before the war and, not unnaturally, followed his master into Rawdon's regiment and was given the rank of ensign. At the fall of Basing House he was imprisoned at Aldersgate and was eventually allowed to retire to France. Returning in 1650 he set up in business at Temple Bar and prospered exceedingly. He did not forget his old master, and when he wrote his treatise on *The Art of Graving and Etching* in 1662, he dedicated it to Peake.

The last of the trio of soldier engravers was Wenceslaus Hollar, whose engravings of Basing House are enlightening, although a trifle fanciful. Born in Prague in 1607 he was intended for the practice of law, but the fortunes of war ruined his family and he was installed as an engraver. By a fortunate chance he was spotted by the Ambassador whilst working in the British Embassy in Prague and when the latter, Thomas Earl of Arundel, returned to England, he took Hollar with him and obtained for him a position in the royal household. When the hostilities commenced he also served at Basing House and at the fall escaped abroad, returning at the Restoration. Alas, instead of prospering as his companions did, his life took a downward trend and he lived in abject poverty. Dying, he beseeched the bailiffs to remove him to no other prison but the grave.

The whole gamut of human emotions and failings can be typified in these glimpses of other characters of the time: we can observe pride in the departure of the stately *Marquis of Newcastle*, who left the country, and with it the King's cause, after the disastrous defeat at Marston Moor, declaring that he would not endure the laughter of the court. *Eythin*, for years bore a grudge against Rupert, and his spite erupted like a lanced boil on the eve of the same battle with the comment, 'By God, Sir, it's very fine in the paper, but there's no such thing in the field', (referring to the Prince's plan of battle sketch). Anguish and sorrow are no newcomers in human experience as may be seen from the spectacle of that hard and stern warrior *Sir Charles Lucas*, who was taken prisoner by the Scots and conducted among the dead to identify them. Even his iron self-control broke down as he gazed upon the pale faces of his fallen comrades, and as the tears rolled down his cheeks he was heard to murmur, 'Alas for King Charles. Unhappy King Charles!' It is relatively easy to be heroic when one is surrounded by heroes and in the heat of the moment, but for sheer cold-blooded valour there is little to match that of trooper *Edward Jeffrey*, who was the messenger for the Marquis of Winchester. It was a commonplace event for him to slip over the walls of Basing House on a foggy night, while the Roundhead army were lying thick round it, with dispatches for Oxford. For an example of greed and treachery there is little to compare with *Sir Richard Grenville*. Amongst the first of Ormond's forces to be sent across from Ireland, he was captured at Liverpool. Straightway he sold his sword to Parliament. Although he had an evil reputation they employed him, as he was an experienced professional, and he later campaigned with Waller in Hampshire and Sussex, becoming a trusted principal officer. However, early in March 1644, he repaid their trust by arriving at Oxford with thirty troopers, £600 of Parliament's money and a coach and six. Possibly more important to the King's cause, he brought knowledge of Waller's strength and a plan to betray Basing House.

In the course of this book, we have endeavoured to relate the fortunes of the common soldier as well as his superiors. We can only get occasional glimpses of how he fared through the medium of anonymous 'Soldiers' Reports', accounts and letters. We see these amateur warriors indulging in small comforts whenever and wherever they found them, grumbling a great deal and facing up to the unpleasantness of any given situation with as much fortitude as they could muster. Many of Wood's entries show they were not basically different from the conscripted soldier of the last war. Does it not ring true when he depicts a Parliamentary soldier airing and warming his boots in front of the fire on a cold November morning? Or when he talks about the evil effects of the life on some 'who are debauched by bearing arms, sitting in tippling houses for whole nights together'? The amateur soldier's thoughts regarding leave and discharge may be seen, plainly stated, in Lieutenant Archer's account of the occasion when, having successfully stormed the town of Alton and inflicted a defeat on the Royalists on 18 December, the London Trained Bands reminded Waller that he had promised their discharge after that action. They desired to be home for Christmas. 'The Lord . . . enabled us to fulfill all our services and brought us home safe to praise his holy name.'[12] Undoubtedly Waller, the professional, did not understand their attitude when there was still work to be done.

In fact Archer is full of naive detail that makes the reader wonder if the Trained Bands did not closely resemble the modern Home Guard as depicted in the popular television programme. We are told that when the order to assemble at Well Close on 16 October 1643 went out the members turned up nonchalantly at all hours until it was so late that the colonel decided nothing could be achieved that day, so they had all better go home and turn out in the better time the next day! But at Brentford they waited two days for the rest of the regiment to turn up, during which some of the men went home and paid substitutes to take their place. Indeed, it would seem that the only factor linking the ancient warrior with the bronze sword and the future soldier with his atomic cannon is the unchanging similarity of man's nature and reactions.

REFERENCES

1. Clarendon VIII p. 168.
2. ibid. VII p. 85.
3. ibid. p. 38.
4. ibid. VIII p. 22.
5. Wood I p. 110.
6. Clarendon VIII p. 169.
7. ibid. v p. 440.
8. ibid. VIII p. 32.
9. ibid. VIII p. 31.
10. ibid. VIII p. 11.
11. ibid. IX p. 134.
12. Archer.

Chapter Nine

Modus Operandi

'It is an ordinary thing in war, to study how to endamage an enemy; and to distract his forces: to which purpose all possible means must be used.'[1]

John Cruso 1632

Compared with the giant set pieces of the battles we have been studying, the day-to-day business of patrols, raids and skirmishes seems small beer indeed. Yet they are an integral part of the war of attrition that was more deadly, vicious, bloody and personal than the field of battle, where armies fought armies with no more than a general animosity to the political attitudes of the opposing side. For example, when some scouts of both sides met between Braddock Down and Lostwithiel on 7 August 1644, so sharp was the clash that Symonds records, 'Four of our foot were killed in fetching in provisions, one more was killed that was sent to fetch in the rambling soldiers.'

Let us then examine 'the little war'. All the varieties of action had one aim, to seek out the enemy whenever he was off guard, to hit him hard and retire after causing as much damage and confusion as possible. The difference, generally speaking, was in the scale of the action. For convenience this can be divided into four categories: the skirmish, the raid, beating up quarters, and outpost duty. With the latter the offensive scope was limited to small ambushes, involving half a dozen men or so, of travellers on the road and so on, but it did contribute to the total aim of spreading alarm and despondency, leading, hopefully, to defeatism in the other side.

THE SKIRMISH

Often this developed into the largest type of action coming within the scope of our chapter heading. It differed from the other types of attack in that both parties were on the warpath, often looking for each other but sometimes meeting by accident. Many times it assumed the proportions of a mini-battle – only the numbers, scale and scope of the major confrontation were missing. So it was at Chalgrove Field on Sunday 18 June 1643. On the previous day there was an alarm that the Roundheads were heading for Islip, five miles from Oxford, to beat up the King's out-quarters, but when the enemy saw the welcome that Sir Arthur Aston and the Lord Wilmot had prepared for them they had second thoughts, and withdrew to Beckley Park and thence into their own quarters. There the matter might well have ended but for Prince Rupert's decision to retaliate, crossing Chislehampton Bridge with 2,000 men, of whom half were horse, 350 dragoons and the rest foot. The van party, who 'marcht like a forlorn hope, a distance before the great partee', consisted of 100 horse and 50 dragoons under Lieutenant-Colonel George Lisle. After some skirmishing in the early hours of Sunday morning, Rupert halted in Chalgrove cornfield about 9 a.m.

'Just at this time we discerned severall great bodyes of the Rebells horse and dragooners coming down Golden Hill towards us from Effington and Tame, who (together with those that had before skirmished in our rear) drew down to the bottom of a great close or pasture ordering themselves amongst the trees beyond a great hedge which parted the close from our field.'[2] Not wishing to have his retreat cut off the Prince secured Chislehampton Bridge. For this purpose Colonel Lunsford and Colonel Washington were sent with the foot to secure the approaches to the bridge and to line the lanes that led to it, the purpose of this last manoeuvre being to lure the Roundheads into a trap. In order to entice them Rupert feigned a retreat. The eager Parliamentarians double-marched towards him and their strength was seen to be 8 cornets of horse plus 100 commanded horse and 100 dragoons.

Soon they were only separated by the hedge. There they faced the Royalists.

Rupert would no longer listen to those who counselled retreat to draw the enemy into an ambush. 'Their insolence is not to be endured,'[3] he snapped, and formed his men for battle. With the dash and daring for which he was famous, he spurred his horse at the hedge and leapt it 'in the face of the dragoons'. The captain (Sir Richard Crane) and the rest of his troop jumped after him and about fifteen got over. The dragoons gave one volley and fled. Meanwhile Lieutenant-Colonel O'Neale, with Prince Rupert's regiment, passed through the end of the hedge and attacked the eight troops. These faced about, having withdrawn a little distance, and gave the Royalists a volley of pistol and carbine shot. 'To say truth they stood our charge of pistols and swords better than ever done since their first beating at Worcester [Powick Bridge].' While this right wing was standing to it manfully the left wing, assaulted by Rupert and the Lifeguard, routed them 'at the first encounter'.

Then all the Roundheads retreated on their reserves of three troops in the grove near Wapsgrove House, which gave way, 'so that all being now in confusion were pursued by ours a full mile and a quarter (as the neighbours say) from the place of the first encounter'. The victorious Cavaliers did not pursue them further because their horses were tired and they had learnt the lesson of Edgehill, 'not to pursue too farre'. The anonymous chronicler states: 'The number of the slain, we cannot yet learn, only we hear that 33 (say some, others 29) were buried in Chalgrove.'

THE RAID

A typical example, not without its humorous side, was the raid planned by Colonel Will Legge, Governor of Oxford, upon Parliamentarian Colonel Richard Greaves, 'a most confiding Presbyterian, laying couchant for a considerable time in Thame with a great partie of horse',[4] designed to stir him out of his complacency. The Royalist force was composed of

400 horse under Colonel David Walter, High Sheriff of Oxfordshire, and Colonel Robert Legge, the Governor's brother, with sixty musketeers. Leaving Oxford on the afternoon of 6 September 1645, they reached Thame about daybreak, 'before any of the rebels were stirring'. They found all the avenues barricaded. Legge's major, Scrope Medcalfe, led the forlorn hope, the enemy's guard were beaten from their posts and Medcalfe and seven of his men 'leapt from their horses and removing the carts opened the avenue'.[5] Many of Greaves's troopers 'came out of their beds into the market-place without their doublets', including Adjutant-General Puide, who fought in his shirt. Those quartered in the vicar's house fled into the church and locked themselves in, some taking their horses with them. A number of the Cavaliers, retiring with their spoils towards their garrison at Boarstall House, 'ran into the vicar's house, and seized on cloaks and goods of the rebels', who were 'beholding out of the church windows what they were doing'. Some of the Parliament troopers had been 'progging for venison' in Thame Park the previous day and had one or two pasties in the oven. Wood records gleefully: 'But so it was, that none of the said rebels were left at eleven of the clock to eat the said pasties, so that their share fell amongst the school-boyes that were sojournours in the said house.'[6]

In this raid the rebels lost 27 officers, many arms, between 200 and 300 good horses, 'and a great deal of money was found in the rebels' pockets (having lately received advance-money)'. This success was not without loss, for Major Medcalfe, who had led the initial charge into the market-place, died of a shot wound in the arm, which would hardly have proved mortal nowadays, and in the last charge Captain Henry Gardiner was shot dead – 'a youth of such high incomparable courage, mix'd with such abundance of modesty and sweetness, that wee cannot easily match him unless with his brave brother, young Sir Thomas Gardiner, which two are now buried both in one grave in the cathedral of Christ Church whether they were brought with much universal sorrow and affection'.

BEATING UP QUARTERS

These pinprick sallies were designed to undermine the enemy's morale and to weaken his resolution, and in this they may well have succeeded. A typical example of this type of attack may be found in Colonel Sir John Urry's expedition to West Wycombe on 25 June 1643. The target was some newly levied troops from Kent and Sussex. Spies had informed Urry that they consisted of 500 foot and one troop of horse but, as a contemporary account states, 'the Lion is never troubled how many the Lambs be', and a force of 200 horse and 40 dragoons were considered adequate for the task. The horse were taken from three different regiments, each party to be commanded by a captain: Sir Thomas Dallison with 70 of Prince Rupert's, Captain Fretzfield with about as many of the Lord Wilmot's, while the remainder, drawn from Sir Arthur Aston's, were under Captain Sebastian Bunklye. The dragoons were commanded by Captain William Tuke.

They left Abingdon on Midsummer day about 7 p.m., arriving at Wycombe about 3 a.m. the next morning. They forced the gates and met a guard of townspeople prepared to shoot. Just what happened to them is not revealed, the report briefly stating that the town was entered 'first by a Corporal and twelve troopers designed for the forlorn hope. Next fell in Sir Thomas Dallison with his troop being seconded by the dragooners who were followed by Captain Fretzfield, the rear being brought up by Captain Bunklye. By these the market-place, streets and all the Avenues being made good, the rest fell to searching the houses for the enemy.' The surprise was complete. Never was panic more complete in a rabbit warren upon the appearance of a ferret than at Wickham that day.

They did not find many Roundheads who stopped to fight. Just one complete troop with 'some other odd troopers and some straggling foote'. At the first alarm the majority of these unseasoned soldiers had bolted straight from their beds just as they were into the woods and the other hiding places, 'some naked, others with doublets, shoes or stockings as their several fears hastened them'. The writer was not without sympathy for their dilemma, for he stated, probably from his own experience, ' 'Tis the terriblest thing in the world to have an enemy fall into one's quarters by night. Nothing resembles more the last Resurrection and Judgement.' Some few, however, did stand and fight, two of whom were killed – 'thereof one scorned quarter from such base dogs, as his dying charity was to say'. Eighty horses were taken with 'their saddles, carbines, pistols and other military furniture'.

The chronicler adds in a very self-satisfied and smug tone, ' . . . and thus the quarter being beaten up and the new troops defeated, the King's Part quietly turned home again . . . undisturbed, by two in the afternoon they all came safe in their own quarters.' The night or early morning attack seems to have been very popular for a good reason as we have seen, but there was not a guaranteed 100 per cent success in these ventures. Sometimes the biter got bitten, as when the large part of the garrison of Basing House set out to trounce (as they thought) the Roundhead outpost at nearby Odiham. It had been previously arranged that two local men would guide the attackers, 'one with a dark lantern and the other with torches to fire the town'.[7] Each man in the party was to have 5 shillings and all the plunder he could carry. Unfortunately, the enemy had been forewarned and, as the Royalist party, consisting of 80 horse and 200 foot, approached through the night-shrouded lanes, they were challenged by a sentry at Warnborough Mill, 'about half a mile from Odiham', who sounded the alarm. Skirmishing broke out with the watch of horse who fell back, probably deliberately. Pressing on they were shortly assaulted flank and front by a vastly superior force of Roundheads. The flank attack was commanded by Colonel Richard Norton, who 'marching very close to the enemy very furiously fell upon them with great valour'.[8] Colonel Samuel Jones, Governor of Farnham Castle, led the frontal attack with his foot. 'The horse came in at the rear, at which all the enemy horse fled and all the foot were taken, the pursuit being almost to Basing House.' The loss severely crippled the defence of the House for they lost some valuable officers, Captain Rowland and his brother, Lieutenant Ivory, Ensign

10. Detail of the battle plan of Naseby from Sprigge's *Anglia Rediviva*

11. Above: 'They stood up and down the field in several bodies of Horse' (*from Hugo's De Militia Equestri Antiqua et Nova, Amsterdam 1630*). Below: A modern re-enactment (by members of the Sealed Knot) of the procedure of preparing a seventeenth-century cannon for firing (*Associated Newspapers Group Ltd*)

Coram and the Marquis of Winchester's personal surgeon, besides 91 other ranks.

Practice alarms may be thought to be a modern device to keep soldiers on their toes and to complicate their existence, but this is not so. 'Sir Ralph Hopton and [Major-General] Sir John Berkeley with a small party of horse and dragoons going about 12 at night to view the guards, being desirous to see how they would receive an alarm, beat in their horse guards and caused the dragoons to fire upon their court of guard whereby they put them into a very confused alarm and finding their temper, alarmed them every night in the like manner as long as they stayed before them.' This was at Sherborne on 7 September 1642. In the profit and loss accounts of the Civil War these attacks seem generally to have been worthwhile if only for the effect on the enemy's nerves and morale.

OUTPOSTS

It was a thankless but most valuable task to be on outpost duty. In any attack the outposts were the first to contact the enemy and, by the smallness of their numbers, were liable to suffer heavily. In how many accounts of the Civil War do we not read the fatal sentence, 'The enemy outposts were driven in'? Yet their vulnerability could be reduced by careful planning. We learn that 'near the Barrow on Cutchinlaw Hill were certain soldiers belonging to the King's garrison in Abingdon, perhaps a dozen or more [probably Sir Lewis Dyves's regiment], that kept watch and guarded themselves in a great pit, thereby, so that if an enemy came there was nothing to be shot at but their heads'. The garrison of Boarstall House often placed an outpost in the vicarage, 'the outhouse northward from Thame'. There they would stay all night, sending some of their party 'to lie in wait for provisions or wine that came from London to Aylesbury or to any persons thereabouts that took part with the rebels'.[9] Some of these troopers, says Anthony Wood, 'would discourse with the school boyes while they were making their exercises in the

Ambush

hall against the next day'. It cannot be denied that a windfall
of creature comforts and necessities came the way of the lucky
soldier in these small affrays, for on 13 August 1644 near
Lostwithiel, 'Sir Jacob Astley tooke two butts of sack [sherry],
much tobacco and horseshoes, etc. coming from Foye to the
enemy'.

OF SPIES

That both sides encouraged spying is obvious. What may
seem odd to us is that this was split into two separate categories, Intelligence and Secret Service. The latter conjures up
James Bondish visions of cloak and dagger activities, but their
pursuits very largely consisted of the spreading of propaganda.
In January 1643 the King authorised the publication of an
official Court Gazette to counter the flood of pamphlets and
bulletins that were being churned out in London by his
enemies, with woeful tales of Royalist atrocities and defeats.

The editor was one John Birkenhead, a man with a vitriolic wit and a master of the derisive phrase, who quickly made the newsheet *Mercurius Aulicus* into a potent weapon. When the Parliament sheets falsely reported the death of Sir Jacob Astley in battle, he was quick with the retort, 'Sir Jacob Astley, lately slain at Gloucester, desires to know was he slain by a musket or a cannon bullet?' Published weekly at Oxford and selling for one penny, they were picked up by these 'secret service agents' at agreed collection points, sometimes by women disguised as beggars, and smuggled into London where the sheets were so much sought after that copies often changed hands at 18 pence! Soon the demand exceeded the supply, which gave rise to another modern-sounding activity. Illicit presses were set up which copied the latest Oxford edition – not always accurately! In addition to *Aulicus* numerous pamphlets were printed and circulated. The large sums recorded on the list reproduced in this chapter proves that the Royalist authorities were fully alive to the danger of the occupation, and large sums were paid to the 'agents'.

That there were persons engaged in what we now consider as spying was proved when the Marquis of Winchester, master of Basing House, who was anxious to discover what new attack the Parliament was preparing against him, sent a servant, Tobias Baisley by name, into London. It seems that he made several successful trips but ventured into the lion's maw once too often. *Mercurius Civicus*, from whose columns this sad tale is taken, relates that Tobias was apprehended, and on 6 February 1644 was tried by a Council of War and sentenced to death. Twelve days later he was taken to Smithfield, 'guarded by Mr Quartermain, the Marshal and divers others of the City officers and a company of the trained bands'. The writer exclaims, with mock surprise, that when the executioner came to do his task the victim 'showed much unwillingness to go off the ladder'!

Symonds shows that the term 'spy' was interpreted as having a very wide meaning and covered even messengers bearing dispatches. 'This day a fellow that was carrying letters from [the Earl of] Essex was taken and hanged below the rendezvous that all the army might see him as they passed by.' The common criterion of spying at any time is the uniform one is, or is not, wearing. If one was carrying dispatches for the King and wearing an orange Parliamentarian sash one might find it difficult to explain to a stern-faced Roundhead sectary that it was all a case of mistaken identity.

Intelligence, of course, is still spying, but in the seventeenth century had a military rather than a political significance. The Scoutmaster was the equivalent of the modern Intelligence Officer, and to him fell the task of locating the enemy, appraising his numbers, composition and assessing his intentions. As we have seen this was far from being a sinecure and must have been a perpetual headache. Little is known of the exact procedure, but the Roundhead Scoutmaster, Sir Samuel Luke, used to send men of his own troop on this work. Obviously he wanted men whom he knew to be reliable to carry out this vital task, and there is no reason why the Royalists should not have done likewise. It may be supposed that the ordinary peasant who came in and reported movements of troops observed during the course of his daily round was encouraged by gifts of money, for all was grist to the mill. In this respect it is listed that 'divers people' received £2 between them.

That there was also a collection of intelligence by special messengers who brought in the reports of garrison commanders to a central point (Oxford) where they must have been collated, is also shown on the list that gives various sums to Sir Arthur Aston, Sir Lewis Dyve, Sir Edward Lydenham and others 'for Intelligence'. The list is given in full:

PAYMENTS FOR INTELLIGENCE BETWEEN I APRIL 1642 AND 26 OCTOBER 1643 (JOHN ASHBURNHAM'S ACCOUNTS)

To the Scoutm[aste]r Generall [(Sir) William Neale]	0050	00	00
To [Captain Francis] Whitehead the Scout[master]	0050	00	00
To divers people for Intelligence	2	00	00
To [Colonel] Sir Lewis Dives [Dyve] for Intelligence [Governor of Abingdon]	0100	00	00

To Sir V[Vivian] M[olineux] for Secret Service	0050	00	00
To [Sergeant-Major-General] Sir Art. Aston for Intelligence	0050	00	00
To 3 gentlemen for Secret Service	0150	00	00
To one employed on Secret Service	0020	00	00
To Mr [ ] Tompkins for Secret Service	0020	00	00
To [ ] Gough for Intelligence	0005	00	00
To Captaine [ ] Morton for Intelligence	0001	00	00
To Sir Edward Sydenham for Intelligence	0001	00	00
To Sir W[ ] G[ ] for Secret Service	0050	00	00

The whole question of spies and spying is summed up very neatly by Cruso[10] who observes: 'The best and principal means for a commander to effect many worthy designs are, first to keep his own deliberations and designs secret. Secondly to penetrate the designs and intentions of the enemy. For which purpose it behoveth him to have good spies which must be exceedingly well rewarded.'

REFERENCES

1. Cruso, *Instructions for the Cavall'rie*, p. 89.
2. *An account of Prince Rupert's . . . Victory in Retreat at Chalgrove on Sunday morning* (anon.), 18 June 1643.
3. ibid.
4. Wood 1 p. 120.
5. ibid. p. 121.
6. ibid. p. 123.
7. Marquis of Winchester's *Siege Diary*, 1644.
8. *A great Victory obtained by Col. Norton . . . over Col. Royden near Walnborough Mill*. Published London 1644.
9. Wood 1 p. 123.
10. *Instructions for the Cavall'rie* p. 81.

Chapter Ten

The Day of Battle

'O Lord! Thou knowest how busy I must be this day.
If I forget thee, do not Thou forget me.'

Prayer of Sir Jacob Astley, Edgehill 1642

No battle can be said to be wholly typical of the warfare of
any period, but a close study of the conduct of the battles of
the Civil War will reveal a certain conformity in the disposition of troops and overall strategy that may be said to be
typical. In this chapter a hypothetical battle is presented in a
composite form, compounded of an amalgam of events from
various engagements, which may be considered to represent
military thought of the time, the structure of the whole resting
loosely on the conduct of Marston Moor. It is composed of
seven phases.

PHASE ONE: ADVANCE TO CONTACT

One of the greatest handicaps of the seventeenth-century
general was his need to seek and find the exact location and
numbers of the enemy. Before Edgehill the two opponents
wandered slowly through the Midlands for a week, each
having only the vaguest idea where the other was.[1] Marching
from Southam to Edgecote on 22 October 1642 the King must
have been perturbed by this lack of intelligence, supposing, as
he probably did, that Essex was marching to block his path to
London. Both sides were on a collision course: it was vital to
have warning when and where it would occur. To this end
Lord Digby was sent out with a party of 400 horse to seek out
the enemy. The tension mounted when he returned and

reported that there was no sign of him. Contact was not established until later that evening when, by chance, quartermasters of the opposing forces clashed at Wormleighton. It would be difficult to say which was the more astonished but the Royalists were the first to recover from the shock, taking prisoners who gave them the first reliable intelligence as to where Essex lay. The Parliamentarian command must have received information speedily but presumably not until the men had dispersed to their quarters. Rupert sent out a scouting party of twenty-four troopers under Lieutenant Clement Martin to Kineton to discover whether Essex had arrived there.[2] He had! Positive contact had been made at last!

PHASE TWO: RECONNAISSANCE AND PLANNING

Reconnaissance is the grist that determines the quality of the tactical loaf. All too often we read that the lack of it, or of a proper appreciation of it, by the opposing commanders had tragic consequences. Some officers learnt their lessons tardily, many never did. More must be known about the enemy's whereabouts than merely that a detachment is in a certain position, before counter measures may be taken. It could well be a feint, as on the occasion when Rupert went to the relief of York. The Allied commanders, aware of their numerical superiority and expecting no guile, 'made ready a welcome for the Prince' by barring the road from Knaresborough to York on the flat heathy ground at Long Marston. However, Rupert's intention was to relieve York and add the numbers of the northern army to his own, thus fighting on more equal terms. To do this he planned to enter the city by the 'back door', and to deceive the enemy at Marston Moor he sent a formidable force of cavalry to face the Allied armies. This seemed to confirm that Rupert was indeed planning a head-on assault on their position. The deception held long enough for the Royalists to seize the bridge of boats at Poppleton and march in, with the Scots and Parliamentarians grinding their teeth in impotent fury.

'If York be lost . . .'

At the first battle of Newbury lack of proper reconnaissance put the Royalist army at a disadvantage, although Sir John Byron said there was still enough light for it.[3] The account attributed to Digby states that they failed to observe a' round hill . . . from whence a battery would command all the plain before Newbury where the King's Army stood'. Byron adds that he marched 'toward a little hill full of enclosures [of] which the enemy (through negligence . . .) had possessed himself'. Before Edgehill both sides seem to have done a little reconnaissance, although the Parliamentarians seem to have been slow to make use of the information their patrols brought in. About midnight Prince Rupert, with the advanced guard, sent to the King who was residing at Sir William Chancie's house at Edgecote the intelligence that the Earl of Essex's headquarters were at Kineton. Charles might have been getting information from a variety of sources, perhaps even from loyal peasants whose local knowledge could be of more value to him than his patrols. Not until 3 a.m. on 23 October did the certain knowledge that the enemy was marching on Banbury arrive. It was apparently Rupert's suggestion that the army should line the heights at Edgehill, for the King sent him this brief message:

Nepheu,

I have given order as you have desyred; so I dout not but all the foot and canon will bee at Egehill betymes this morning, where you will also find

Your loving oncle & Faithful frend

Charles R.

4 o'clock this Sunday morning.

The planning of the battle array was simplified by their position, from where, as from the grandstand, the arena could be seen. Looking down on Kineton they could see 'the Rebel Army drawing themselves out and setting themselves in Battalia'. The King, using a perspective glass (telescope), 'took view of Essex's army in the vale about a mile distant'. Prince Rupert must have made a sketch of what he conceived the Royalist battle should be, the fair copy of which we have in de Gomme's plan. He did the same thing for Marston Moor. At both battles the Royalist High Command quarrelled over the order of battle, the formation of the troops and over rank and precedence. Both Lindsey, as Lord General, and Rupert, as General of the Horse, were jealous of their position and their powers. Lindsey's advice on the advance, given in the interests of the foot, may have been disregarded in favour of Rupert's, which had been given in the interests of the horse. In the discussion of the order of battle Lindsey, with some justification, refused to allow Rupert to direct the ordering of the infantry in the field. Rupert retorted that the battle could not be planned piecemeal and, moreover, insisted that pikemen and musketeers be interspersed with each other in the Swedish fashion. The King took the advice of his favourite nephew. The Earl of Lindsey's resentment flared into rage. Casting his baton of command on the ground in front of the assembled generals he said, 'Since your Majesty thinks me not fit to perform the office of Commander-in-Chief I would serve you as colonel only', and went and placed himself at the head of his regiment of foot. Rupert, saturnine, proud and tactless, was to have this effect on many of his associates, for he was engaged in just such another planning session on the eve of Marston Moor when he was rebuffed by Lord Eythin, military adviser to the Marquis of Newcastle, neither of whom were in favour of giving battle at that time. 'Sir,' said Eythin, bringing up an old grudge, 'your forwardness lost us the day in Germany when you yourself were taken prisoner.' It might seem that at Marston Moor the Parliamentarian Command, with fewer professional soldiers in their number, were much more in accord. 'General Lesley [Lord Leven] gave order for drawing up the battle', we are told, and it is obvious that the other commanders, Manchester and Lord Fairfax, both amateurs, were only too pleased to give the supreme command to a soldier who had had thirty years of service in the Swedish army, then the foremost in Europe. There are some indications that at Edgehill Essex, also, could rely on the trust and obedience of his officers as well as having an undivided command. He had few senior officers.

PHASE THREE: THE ORDER OF BATTLE

The argument at the planning session was largely concerned with the order in which the men should fight. Those who had seen service in Sweden favoured the methods of Gustavus Adolphus, whose tactics had been so original and successful that men still talked of him with awe when he had been ten years in his grave. Others, used to the more simple procedure of the Dutch army, felt that with largely untrained and inexperienced men this was the ideal. The young Duke of York witnessed the whole embarrassing scene as Dutch and Swedish schools fought their bloodless skirmish with rising tempers and fiery phrases, as he was to testify later. With Sir Jacob Astley installed as commander of the foot, the ordering of the field was concluded. As the Roundheads showed no intention of charging up the steep slope the Royal army descended to the base to give their cavalry more breathing space. When their army was deployed the cavalry was on the wings. Those on the right under Rupert were the Lifeguard, the Prince of Wales's, Prince Rupert's, Prince Maurice's and Sir John Byron's regiments at an approximate strength of 1,695 men, all except Byron's in the first line. Those on the left under Lord Wilmot were his own regiment, Lord Grandison's, the Earl of Carnarvon's, Lord Digby's and Sir Thomas Aston's, amounting to approximately 1,055 men, all

The plan of attack

save Aston's and Digby's in the first line. De Gomme's plan shows the foot drawn up in five brigades. According to him sixteen regiments composed this force. As we have already seen their equipment, weapons and even experience differed greatly.

The brigade commanders were, starting from the left wing, Henry Wentworth, Richard Feilding's and Charles Gerard, with, forming a second line, Sir Nicholas Byron and John Belasyse. All these gentlemen had colonel's rank, all save Byron and Wentworth were regimental commanders. Of the three regiments of dragoons, two were on the left wing under Sir Arthur Aston and Sir Edmund Duncombe, while the third on the right was commanded by Colonel James Usher. Clarendon tells us that 'the Earl [Essex] with great dexterity performed whatsoever could be expected by a wise general. He chose the ground that best liked him. There was between the hill and the town a fair campania, save that near the town it was narrower and on the right hand side some hedges and enclosures.'[4] He was determined to play a waiting game, if only because his army was by no means all assembled. As many as three regiments of foot and eleven troops of horse and not fewer than seven guns would be expected to catch up with his main body by the morrow. So he stood and waited to be assaulted.

The left wing commander Sir James Ramsey gives us a good idea of the tactics of the times with this description of his preparations at Edgehill:[5] 'I did accordingly put them [the soldiers] in Posture offensive and Defensive, interlining the squadrons with a convenient number of musketeers.' Three hundred musketeers were placed in a hedge, 'which did flank the whole front of the left wing'. Ramsey had also seen Swedish service and like his opponents was putting into practice what he had learnt. On Ramsey's right and to his rear were four regiments which formed Charles Essex's brigade. Once again the difference between officers who had seen Dutch and Swedish service was apparent, for these men, who formed a single line, had fallen in in the eight ranks customary in the Dutch army, a simple array that the Lord General (the Earl of Essex) was also known to favour. Ballard's brigade was behind that of Charles Essex. On the right of the foot was Meldrum's brigade with three regiments in line and that of Sir William Fairfax in the rear. A single regiment of horse under Lord Feilding was on the right, supported, it is supposed, by 700 dragoons 'in the bushes to make a show'. It was afternoon before both armies were in position.

PHASE FOUR: ASSAULT

The most nerve-racking time for the common soldier is when he is at action stations waiting for something to happen. The officers, being fully occupied with planning and a host of other details, have little time to contemplate the more unpleasant aspects of the immediate future, but the 'Tommy' of the time had ample time to gaze upon the enemy's preparations, to see the twinkle of his armour, the brightness of his banners, the ominous muzzles of his cannon with all their implications, and it can be a gut-twisting experience which doubtless has altered little in 300 years. Possibly the longest wait the armies had was at Marston Moor, when for four hours they stood and faced each other in the damp afternoon heat. The Roundheads sang psalms and hymns to pass the time. The sound of their own voices and the martial words

Charge for horse!

of the old chants, coupled with their religious fanaticism, raised their spirits high. By 4 p.m. on 2 July 1644, both armies were fully deployed, but no one made a move. By 7 p.m. Rupert had decided that it was too late to commence that day. Smoke from a multitude of cooking fires started to rise as the Royalists began to prepare their evening meal. Through their perspective glasses the Parliamentarian commanders could see troopers dismounting, pikemen at their ease. Even Rupert had gone to the rear to partake of supper, while the Marquis of Newcastle had retired to the comfort of his coach to smoke a pipe. Now was the best time to attack, while the enemy was off guard.

A cannon fired the signal to advance. Suddenly the whole Allied army, horse, foot and dragoons, began to move down the slope, the foot moving, not at their regulation seventy paces to the minute, but at a running march. It needs little imagination to conjure up the consternation of the Royalist musketeers and pikemen, intent on their culinary tasks, when they saw the enemy on the move and coming straight for them. However, despite this initial advantage all did not go well with the Roundheads. On the right, Sir Thomas Fairfax's horse, obstructed by broken ground and furze, was eventually routed by Lord George Goring. Sir Charles Lucas's brigade of horse, once Fairfax's horse was shattered, went on to assault the foot. Confusion spread down the Allied line and many began to retreat. On the left wing things were going equally amiss for the Royalists. Cromwell's charge had the impact of a battering-ram, and in a short time the men of Byron's command were routed. The fearsome, reckless and arrogant Prince Rupert, seeing them flee, put himself at the head of his reserve, and as they galloped by, shouted at them, 'zounds, do you flee? Follow me.' Evidently more afraid of him than the enemy, they formed behind him and charged again. The Ironsides 'had a hard pull of it, they were charged by Rupert's bravest men both flank and front. They stood at sword's point a pretty while hacking at each other, but at last (it so pleased God) he broke through scattering them before him like a little dust.'[6]

It seems likely that the balance was turned in the favour of Parliament by the attack of the Scots cavalry under David Leslie. Less well mounted than Cromwell's men, they lacked the impact of the Ironsides and at one time must have winced from Rupert's horse; but fresh men appearing at a time when both sides were tiring had a decisive effect. The Royalist cavalry was routed and Rupert himself, cut off from his Life-guard, was forced to hide in a bean field for his life. This is a positive kind of assault with a positive kind of result – warfare at its most simple and direct. Affairs were not always as clear-cut as this, however. James II, as a boy, was at Edgehill, and describes a situation where both sides reached stalemate, and unable to break their opponents at push of pike, became involved in a prolonged fire fight. 'The foot being thus engaged in such warm and close service it were reasonable to imagine one side should run and be disordered but it happened otherwise, for each as though by mutual consent retired some few paces and they struck down their colours, continuing to fire at each other even until night.'

A dragoon gets his man

Sometimes, particularly in the early stages of the war, one gets instances of the normal instincts of self-preservation overriding the cold brain and steel nerves of the soldier. At Chewton on 10 June 1643 Captain Atkyns charged with 100 men, and when he came to reform there were not 30 left. Three fresh troops of the enemy were forming to oppose them in their rear, preventing them from reaching their own lines. 'I told those of my party, that if we did not put a good face on it and charge them presently [i.e. immediately] before they were in order, then we were all dead men or prisoners, which they apprehending, we charged them and they made as it were a lane for us, being as willing for us to be gone as we ourselves.'[7] Although cannon were never available in sufficient numbers to be a decisive factor they blanketed the field with rolling clouds of powder smoke and largely, one guesses, were more nuisance than they were worth, their full potential only being realised in siege warfare. Nevertheless their contribution should not be belittled. Sergeant Henry Foster of the Red Regiment of the London Trained Bands relates how at First Newbury they found themselves opposite the main Royalist battery of eight guns 'far less than twice musket distance away'. Naturally, the Royalist gunners were delighted with such a target and 'did some execution at first and were somewhat dreadful when men's bowels and brains flew in our faces, but blessed be God that gave us courage so that we kept our ground and after a while feared them not'. Although these are the words of a Roundhead undoubtedly the Royalist foot had similar feelings.

Obviously there are endless permutations of the assault. The Duke of York (later James II) commented:

> The naturell courage of English men, which prompted them to maintain their ground, tho' the rawness and unexperience of both parties had not furnished them with skill to make the best use of their advantages. 'Tis observed that of all nations the English stick closest to their Officers and tis hardly seen that our common Soldiers will turn their backs, if they who commanded them do not set them the bad example,'[8]

PHASE FIVE: THE CRISIS

The overwhelming difficulty of command under the circumstances of seventeenth-century warfare is plainly shown when we are told that after a charge by enemy horse a commander 'peered long and earnestly through the smoke clouds to make out if indeed they had gone before ordering the advance'. This confusion is underlined by a letter written by Arthur Trevor who rode with dispatches for Rupert from Skipton to Marston Moor: 'I could not meet the Prince until the battle was joined and in the fire, smoke and confusion of that day I knew not for my soul where to incline . . . not a man being able to give me the least hope where the Prince was to be found.'[9] Not surprising, for as we can see, the general who stayed in his command post (Rupert's was marked by a

12. Pass issued by Charles I at Oxford in 1646 (*Hereford City Library*)

13. Sir Henry Gage (*British Museum*)

Dispatches for the general

banner 5 yards long) ran the risk of losing touch with the action. It seems that once the fighting had begun much had to be left to the initiative of the tertia commanders who had had the overall strategy of the battle explained to them beforehand, and the whole outcome sometimes pivoted on the 'on the spot' decision of a colonel. Thus Rupert galloped off to the right wing while Newcastle decided to look to the centre. It was a scene of confusion, and 'as he was hastening to see what posture his own regiment was he met with Sir Thomas Metham and his troop and after a short harangue he [Newcastle] led them to the charge'.

In the majority of battles there comes a moment of crisis when one side falters. It may not be the end, but it may be pinpointed afterwards as the moment when the battle was decided. Hence at Cheriton it can be said that the crisis occurred when the Parliamentarian Major-General Browne collected 100 musketeers from hedges and fired a murderous volley into the wavering, but not yet routed, Royalist cavalry.

They started to wheel and 'a hot charge from our horse forced them to a disorderly retreat'.[10] Five hundred musketeers left the shelter of the hedges, advancing with speed so that the Royalist foot, who had stood to it all day, 'perceiving their horse begin to fly do seek shelter by flight themselves and to throw away their arms'. At Naseby it may be thought that the critical moment came when Astley's left flank was exposed and Cromwell unleashed the bulk of his command against it. Seeing this, the King was about to counter-attack in person with his Lifeguards and some of the Newark Horse. 'At this moment,' says James Walker, the King's Secretary, 'the King's Horseguards, and the King at the head of them were ready to charge those who followed ours, when a person of quality, 'tis said the Earl of Carnwarth, took the King's horse by its bridle, turning him about, swearing at him and saying "Will you go upon your death?" and at the same time the command was given "March to your right hand" which (as most concluded) was a civil command for everyone to shift for himself.' The chance was missed and Charles's hesitancy cost him his crown and brought him that much closer to the headsman's block in Whitehall. At Marston Moor the moment of crisis was probably when Rupert's horse broke and he himself was so nearly taken or killed. To avoid the turning of the Royalist flank the surviving regiments had to wheel and by nightfall had assumed a position almost at right angles to their original position.

PHASE SIX: MOPPING UP

Manchester's army then attacked, while Cromwell, advancing between Wilstrop Wood and White Syke Close, 'met with the enemy's horse (being retreated upon the repulse they had from the Scottish foot) at the same place of disadvantage where they had routed our horse formerly'. These were the cavalry of Lord Goring who had initially been successful against Fairfax's horse. After the dispersal of Goring's force Cromwell, with Leslie and Fraser, assaulted the rear of the Royalist troops who still stood firm. The Parliamentarian

A parley

forces at this stage did not meet with any great resistance until they came to the Marquis of Newcastle's battalion of White-coats,

> . . . who first peppering them with shot, when they came to charge stoutly bore them up with their pikes that they could not enter to break them. Here the Parliament horse of that wing received their greatest loss and a stop for some time to their hoped for victory, and that only by the stout resistance of this gallant battalion which consisted near of four thousand foot . . . when all their ammunition was spent, having refused quarter, every man fell in the same order and rank wherein he had fought.[11]

Captain Camby in his eye-witness account confirms the desperate valour of these Whitecoats who had sworn to dye their coats in the blood of the enemy, and adds that 'he never met such resolute brave fellows or those he pitied so much . . . he saved the lives of two or three against their will'. In a like manner one tertia (possibly Lisle's) resisted beyond the call of duty at Naseby, 'standing with incredible courage and resolution',[12] resisting Cromwell's attacks from all sides. It took the combined assault of Commander-in-Chief Fairfax and General Cromwell to crush these stubborn fellows.

PHASE SEVEN: PURSUIT AND SPOILS

Once broken, the soldiers of those times – who, after all, were civilians at heart – tended to run and keep running. After Cheriton the lane from Sutton Scrubbs to the village was supposed to have run with blood as the Kentish men slaughtered without mercy the Redcoats of Lord Inchiquin's regiment, who were the first of the King's men to break. Local tradition has it that when Balfour's and Heselrige's cavalry caught up with the fleeing infantry after three or four miles, the foot shouted to the Royalist remnants of horse, 'Face them, for God's sake, face them again.'[13] The suicidal attempt by the battle-worn cavalry brought them only a few more minutes of life before the horsemen were amongst them. The pursuit was pressed so vigorously that Sir William Balfour delayed writing his report on the battle until the next day, so desperate was he for sleep. After Naseby the pursuit of the fugitives was pressed as far as Leicester, Cromwell's troopers maliciously killing 100 soldiers' wives and others, 'some of them of quality'. At Edgehill the Royalists charged and broke the Parliamentarian brigade commanded by Charles Essex who fled, panic-stricken. Carried away by the madness and exhilaration of the chase all but three troops of Rupert's horse thundered off in pursuit of the fleeing Roundheads. Through Kineton and beyond they went, many stopping to plunder the baggage train but some, who presumably were enjoying the chase too much to think of profit, did not stop until they ran into an enemy brigade coming up from War-wick, when it was their turn to retire hastily.

At the beginning of this chapter the attitudes of the common soldier and the high ranking officer were contrasted. Hardened by the gulf of inheritance, environment and descent they were almost two separate races. Even in the matter of spoils they had their own ideas of what was import-ant. At the intaking of Basing House Cromwell noted only what was of military importance: 'We have taken ten pieces of ordinance, and much ammunition. We have as prisoners the Marquis [of Winchester], Sir Robert Peake and divers other officers. . . . '14 The point of view of the common man may be said to be represented by the catalogue of spoil pub-lished in the news-sheet *Mercurius Veridicus* (number 25), which included such things as 'the Marquis's plate worth £5,000, Sir Robert Peake's box of jewels, rings and bracelets, a great quantity of wine, many hogsheads of beer'. That is not to say, of course, that a good officer, then as now, does not think of his men's welfare, for Hopton states that at Stratton field 'they took likewise all their cannon being . . . 13 pieces of brasse ordinance and a brasse mortar piece and all their ammunition being seventy barrels of powder . . . and a very great magazine of Bisquette and other provisions and all dis-posed of in very excellent order which was a very seasonable blessing to the Cornish army that had suffered very great want of food for three or four days before'. We may be sure that, for once, the general and the pikeman had their priorities in the same order.

REFERENCES

1. Clarendon vi p. 79.
2. ibid. vi p. 82.
3. Digby's account.
4. Clarendon vi p. 82.
5. Sir James Ramsay, *The Vindication and Clearing of* . . . , Thomason Tracts 669.
6. Scoutmaster-General Lionel Watson's account.
7. Atkyns/Gwyn p. 15.
8. See Bibliography.
9. Arthur Trevor to the Marquis of Ormonde, 10 July 1644.
10. Balfour's dispatch.
11. Lt.-Col. James Somervell's account.
12. Sprigge, *Anglia Rediviva*.
13. Quoted from *Love Loyalty* by Emberton.
14. Cromwell's report to Speaker Lenthall.

Chapter Eleven

After the Fight

Let who can have the day with your favour.
Both Armies are losers for their labours.
Much precious blood is lost many a poor soul.

Stephen Buckley 1643

'It is fortunate that war is so terrible, else we might get too fond of it,' remarked General Robert E. Lee during the American Civil War, and indeed there could be few more terrible sights than the field after a seventeenth-century battle where most of the action was hand-to-hand combat. Arthur Trevor[1] wrote of 'very great execution' at Marston Moor, and Captain Robert Clarke[2] stated that the battle fell heavily on Prince Rupert's old soldiers and the gentry. It seems that here the Royalists lost a third of their force.

To get a clear idea of the slaughter one has only to examine the casualty lists of the Civil War battles. At Edgehill, out of 10,000 foot about 2,500 were lost by the Royalists. At First Newbury Rupert lost 30 of his troop and about 300 of his regiment. Byron lost 100 from his regiment, in other words, a quarter of his strength. At Naseby the cavalry lost 100 officers and gentlemen. The progress of the battle could well be traced by the lines of the dead – the ranks of Yorkshire Whitecoats at White Syke Close, the dreadful tangle of horse and man where Cromwell's Ironsides had been at hand-strokes with Rupert's Cavaliers, the lanes the cannon had carved in the ranks . . . . After First Newbury, Ensign Gwyn saw 'upon the heath . . . a whole file of men six deep with their heads struck off with one cannon shot of ours'.[3] There would not be a lack of people on the field despite these harrowing sights. After Marston Moor the country folk came to bury the dead for reasons of health as well as more avaricious motives. They buried 4,550 in White Syke Close and along the edge of Wilstrop Wood. Of these it has been estimated that 3,000 were Royalist. It would be unlikely that the peasants would be squeamish about removing the purses, rings and even the fine clothes of the dead. Many others would come seeking the bodies of relatives to remove and decently bury them. At least one gentleman owed his life to these two factors and the coldness of the night. Sir Gervase Scroope[4] survived no fewer than sixteen wounds at Edgehill by reason of the fact that the battlefield ghouls, taking him for dead, stripped him and left him naked. The keen overnight frost is supposed to have staunched the flow of blood and next morning his son Adrian carried him off and he recovered, though he always had to carry one arm in a sling.

THE WOUNDED

Robert Wiseman (?1622–76) was one of the great Royalist surgeons. He saw service in the west and was captured at Worcester in 1651. His book *A Treatise of Wounds* was published in 1672 when he was one of Charles's eleven Sergeant-Chirurgeons, and while it may be considered to represent high level medical practice of the day the treatment seems of a rather rough and ready but thoroughly practical variety that took little account of the patient's agony. For instance he recommends, 'If the weapon be stuck in the bone move it up and down to loosen the point then pluck it out, but in case it will not move cut away the bone before you extract it.'

The book's nineteen chapters prescribe treatment for different types of wounds, including those from gunshot, in which the removal of the ball is seen as a necessity: 'Consequently the omission of that extraction will bring mortification which has been the cause of all the mischief the wound is subject to, inflamation, spasms, convulsions and Gangrene.' Wiseman recommends three types of stitching, including the 'glover's stitch' with which he had 'seen the Spaniards draw wounds very close'.

But while the book gives interesting glimpses of the state of medical knowledge of the time, and even an intimation of a faltering step or two in the direction of antiseptic care of wounds, it is a surgeon's handbook written for surgeons, and gives little indication to the historian of the general attitude to, and the kind of treatment that might be expected by, the lesser ranks in the field. We get a better insight into this from a book of *Observations on the Duties of a Regimental Surgeon*, published in the following century by one Robert Hamilton MD. At this time the surgeon seems to have been classed among the lower strata of society, for the author terminates his foreword by saying that he writes it that 'the office of surgeon should gain more respectability'.

This reputation was not altogether undeserved, as is shown by the case of Captain Henry Bellingham. After Edgehill he was 'found amongst the dead, and brought off by his friends with twenty wounds, who after ten days died at Oxford by the negligence of his surgeons, who left a wound in his thigh, not dangerous in itself, undiscerned, and so by festering destroyed a body very hopefully recovered'. Hamilton describes the soldier patient of his era as 'frequently destitute of almost everything fit for his situation, destitute of a proper bed to lie on, destitute of suitable lodgings, destitute of proper food or cordials . . . and in short destitute of everything he should have'. And this at a time when the army was placed upon an organised footing; how much more grim must have been the case of a Royalist soldier in that makeshift army.

The surgeon goes on to state an attitude of mind that he deplored but which seems to have existed amongst the majority of his contemporaries, that medicines 'should be of a cheaper sort . . . and they may be only of a coarser quality since they are only for soldiers, men little accustomed to delicate living or nice medicines . . . if the general tendency of operations be the same, the same effects must unquestionably follow . . . for though he lives low yet nature has formed him with organs as nice and as mobile as his richer neighbour'.[5] After reading the account of operations performed by this qualified surgeon one understands very well how Oliver

Cromwell's nephew died of an amputation after Marston Moor. The general's letter[6] to the bereaved father comes straight to the point: 'It [a cannon shot] brake his leg. We were necessitated to have it cut off, whereof he died.' Lacking antiseptics, anaesthetics, sterilised instruments and all the basics of modern surgery, it is a wonder that any of them survived. To quote our army surgeon again, 'Cool, steady intrepidity where never the heart do fail nor the hand do shake is of all things most required . . . awkwardness is only overcome by repetition . . . surgeons have been known to commence operations and for want of sufficient courage to yield the knife to another.'[7] One forms the opinion that the surgeon's lancet was more to be feared than the Roundhead's sword.

An important part of the equipment was the medicine chest. In it were liniments, syrups, electuaries, antimonials, mercurials, neutral salts and a great many other things. Such curious ingredients as linseed (no proper substitute for olive oil), Peruvian bark (very expensive), rhubarb, and a drink made from marsh mallow roots are mentioned. It might seem that the physician of the time had to be something of a botanist and indeed the garrison of Basing House were very fortunate to have in their midst a very famous botanist and herbalist, Lieutenant-Colonel Thomas Johnson, who was killed during a skirmish in 1644.

While we have observed that the best Royalist surgeon was Robert Wiseman, the best known doctor with the King was William Harvey, the discoverer of the circulation of the blood and the first to state that the heart was the central life support system, rather than the liver, as was the accepted idea in medical circles of that time. The fact that so many did survive amputations is to be attributed to the sturdiness of their physique rather than the skill of the surgeon.

PRISONERS OF WAR

It was quite often a dangerous thing to surrender during a battle as it was a moot point whether quarter would be granted. For instance when Major Robinson threw down his arms at the intaking of Basing House he was shot by a fanatical Puritan officer who exclaimed, 'Cursed be he that doeth the Lord's work negligently!'[8] Even if surrender was accepted one might be worse off than before. Wood describes an occasion when 'the captive parlament soldiers . . . were brought into Oxford over Southbridge, bound and led with matches (whereat there was mutch shoutinge) & conveyed into some place or prison'.[9] Like as not they were without coats for the dead and living were plundered indiscriminately, although in many cases the officers endeavoured to stop it and the King forbade it. 'Yet notwithstanding, our officers did perpetually beat off our foot, many of them lost their hats, etc.'

The prisoner of war seems to have been considered fair game for everyone. The army that surrendered at Lostwithiel, having run the gauntlet of the victorious Royalists, was attacked by the inhabitants. Such incidents were not unusual. They were accepted as commonplace, as something that was undesirable but unavoidable.

Colonel Crawford captures a fleeing Cavalier

As we have seen earlier, prisoners were often inadequately housed and fed. They were often put to work – digging defences, for example, or given a chance to join the Royalist forces. In Oxford on 6 February 1643 the King viewed 'the prisoner captives, to the number of about eleven hundred . . . as they came in, most of them being able and lusty fellows'.[10] After being dispersed to various places of imprisonment next morning, 'some of the properest fellowes of them after they had taken the new protestation appointed lately by his majestie were new apparelled and tooke into service for his majestie'.[11] The only other fate for the prisoner was to be exchanged. It must have been bad for the ego of an officer who thought himself of value to be bartered for, say, two sergeants and five ordinary soldiers; but at the same time it must have saved many from the sin of false pride. There are countless examples of this activity, for example after Cropredy Bridge we learn that 'a trumpet of Waller's came and exchanged sixty and odd prisoners of ours taken by them, which were all they took, we having a hundred more'.[12] The siege diary of the Marquis of Winchester states that on 2 October 1644, 'We sent forth Captain Rosewell and Captain Rigby with instructions to treat for prisoners. The same night Mr Greaves and Captain Jarvis [Jervoise], next day two Lieutenants with divers more sent out receiving Captain Rowlett, a Lieutenant and two sergeants lost at Odiham and some days after Cornet Bryan and three gentlemen of our relief released to Oxford.'

HONOURS AND AWARDS

As we have seen the King was always impecunious so he turned for rewards for his veterans not to gold but to the privilege of rank. In those days elevation to the peerage or a knighthood meant a very great deal, and it was an economical way of rewarding services rendered. In his financial extremity it is true that Charles did offer a nobleman a marquisate for the rather stiff price of £20,000 but these honours were none the less coveted. Sometimes he seems to have created knights in a pure fit of relief and joy at some good tidings, as when Captain Thomas Gardiner of Prince Rupert's regiment of horse 'was knighted by his majesty whilst he sat at dinner, upon the delivery of the news of Prince Rupert's success against the rebels that had besieged Newark'. In one case at least he rewarded the wrong man, in the opinion of one of the onlookers. After Cropredy Bridge 'Lieutenant-Colonel Hooper, of dragoons, [was] knighted, per mistake, Thelwall did the service'.[13] But many who were honoured won it the hard way, like Captain John Smith who rescued the captured royal standard at Edgehill. He had spied the Roundheads carrying it away and, rapier in hand, had rushed in crying, 'Traitor, deliver the standard!'[14] Although wounded, he killed one Parliamentarian, hurt another and routed the rest, who fled, leaving the standard in his possession. No less well deserved was the knighthood gained by Colonel Henry Gage, who forced his way through the encircling forces of Colonel Richard Norton to relieve Basing House, having marched through forty miles of enemy held territory. A list of some of those honoured follows:

PEERAGES

Prince Rupert (1619–1682)	Earl of Holderness and Duke of Cumberland January 1644
Earl of Forth (?1573–1651)	Earl of Brentford 1644
Lord Bernard Stuart (?1623–1645)	Earl of Litchfield 1645

BARONS

Sir John Byron K.B. (d. 1652)	1643 of Rochdale
Sir Jacob Astley (1579–1652)	1644 of Reading
John Belasyse (1614–1689)	1645 of Worlaby
Charles Gerard (d. 1649)	1645 of Brandon

KNIGHTS
1642

James, Duke of York	Earl of Carnarvon	Lord D'Aubigny
Lord John Stuart	Lord Bernard Stuart	Brian Palmes
James Pennyman	Edmond Duncombe	John Digby
Robert Stapleton	Capt. Richard Crane	Col. Thomas Byron
Arnold de Lille	Major Richard Wyllis	Richard Byron

Anthony Morgan
Capt.-Lieut. Robert
    Walsh

Richard Shuckburgh
Wingfield Bodenham
Thomas Blackwell

Lieut. John Smith
Edward Sydenham

1643

Lt.-Col. Henry
    Huncks
Edward Hyde
Col. John Urry
Lt.-Col. Charles
    Compton

Capt. William
    Mallory
Henry Hunloke
Col. Thomas
    Tyldesley
Major William
    Compton
Col. Marmaduke
    Rawdon

William Neale
Lewis Kirke
Lt.-Col. Francis
    Butler
Capt. Spencer
    Compton

1644

Col. John Knotsford
Capt. William
    Ratcliff
Capt. Anthony
    Waldron

Sgt.-Major-General
    Joseph Wagstaff
Lt.-Col. John Boys
James Croft

Capt. Thos.
    Prestwick
Lt.-Col. Anthony
    Greene

1645

Lord Capel
Lt.-Col. George
    Boncle

Charles Cotterell
Major William
    Bridges
Cornet John
    Walpole
Henry Wroth
Col. George Lisle
Major William
    Byron

Lt.-Col. Henry
    Chichely
Edward Walker

Bartholomew
    La Roche
Lt.-Col. Robert
    Peake
Lt.-Col. William
    Leighton
Capt. Theophilus
    Gilby
Capt. Charles Lee
Lt.-Col. James
    Bridgeman

Major Richard
    Hatton
Col. Stephen
    Hawkins
Col. Richard Page
Col. Herbert
    Lunsford
Col. Barnaby
    Scudamore
Edward Cooper
Lt.-Col. Thomas
    Shirley

Following the precedent of Elizabeth I, whose Armada medal bore on one side a relief of the sovereign and on the other a representation of an island with high winds and a stormy sea, with an inscription which, translated, read, 'He blew and they were scattered', Charles also issued commemorative medals to his officers and men. One early medal, produced by Thomas Bushell, was the Forlorn Hope. This met with the sovereign's full approval, as is shown by a royal letter of 12 June mentioning 'your invention for our better knowing and rewarding the Forlorn Hope with Badges of Silver'.[15] Besides the aforementioned Sir John Smith, medals were also won by Sir Thomas Tyldesley, as can be seen in his portrait, and by Sir Robert Walsh, who 'did also in the same manner wear a green ribband with a Medal but whether it was given to him by Order, I do not know'.

Another convenient form of reward, particularly acceptable to those with academic pretensions, was the giving of honorary degrees. Between 1 November 1642 and the following February, 140 MAs were created at the request of the King, until the University felt bound to petition him to desist, not the least of their complaints being that it lowered the standing both of the degree and the University. Perhaps Charles – or one of his advisers – was a shrewd appraiser of the vanity and conceit of human nature, for another of the rewards granted, which was designed to appeal to the ego rather than the pocket, was an augmentation of arms. Dr Edward Lake, a 'professed lawyer', who had thrown off his gown and donned a buff coat, fought at Edgehill and received sixteen wounds. The King was so taken with Lake's spirit that not only was he made a baronet, but received

. . . a coat of Augmentation to be borne before his own: in a field gules, a right arm arm'd, carrying upon a sword a banner argent, charged with a cross between sixteen shields, four in each quarter of the first and in the umbelique point one of our own lions of England. And for a crest to the same coat of augmentation: a chevalier in a fighting position his left arm hanging down useless and holding a bridle in his teeth, his scarf red, his sword, face, armes and horse cruentated.[16]

'Old soldiers never die', they say, and the last survivor of Edgehill was William Hasland, who at the age of 111 was granted a Chelsea pension on 15 February 1731 – eighty-nine years afterwards! Other long-lived survivors were Sir Henry Newton (1618–1701), who was Lieutenant-Colonel to Lord Capel, Marcus Trevor, and Charles, Prince of Wales. Major William Beaw, later to become a bishop, did not die until 1705, while the *London Daily Post* of 19 July 1736 reported that William Walker of Alston, a Cavalier soldier who was wounded at Edgehill and had two horses killed under him, lived to be 122! How much free beer he must have gained by telling toothless tall tales of the action to the habitues of the local tavern! He was buried at Ribchester on 16 January 1736.[17]

REFERENCES

1. Letter to the Marquess of Ormonde, 10 July 1644.
2. Letter to Captain Bartlett from aboard the Parliament ship *Joceline*, 14 July 1644.
3. Atkyns/Gwyn p. 53.
4. Young.
5. Hamilton p. 252.
6. Cromwell to Col. Valentine Walton, 5 July 1644.
7. Hamilton p. 203.
8. Emberton p. 88.
9. Wood 1 p. 73.
10. ibid.
11. ibid.
12. Symonds's diary p. 25.
13. ibid.
14. Edward Walsingham's account.
15. Ellis's *Original Letters*, 2nd series, III p. 309.
16. *The Camden Miscellany* IV, 1859.
17. According to Tom C. Smith and the Rev. J. Shortt, (*History of Ribchester*, 1890, pp. 258–9), there was then a portrait of Walker at Tabley Hall, Cheshire, which showed him wearing his own hair, a large beard and a greatcoat, and holding a walking-stick in his left hand.

14. The fifth Marquis of Winchester (*by permission of the Hon. P. C. Orde Paulet MA*)

15. James Stanley, Earl of Derby (*engraving from a portrait by Van Dyck*)

Chapter Twelve

Besieged

My years had not amounted full eighteen,
Till I in field wounded three times had been,
Three times in sieges close had been immured,
Three times imprisonment's restraint endured.

Anthony Cooper, *Stratologia*, 1662

It was King Charles's misfortune that many of his most powerful subjects wanted to help him on their own terms and in their own back yards, rather than on the larger stage of the national scene. Generally this help consisted of declaring for the King, pulling up the drawbridge of their ancestral castle, or closing the gates of their manor house, and defying the Parliament to do anything about it. The castle, with its mighty keep and massive walls, had long since outlived its usefulness as an effective military installation. The fall of Constantinople with its famous fortifications in 1453 had really marked the beginning of the end for these old style defences against an enemy with cannon in his siege train, while the manor house had seldom been built from a military viewpoint in the first place. We have seen, however, that the arts of war had to be learnt by the majority, and the shortage of equipment made the holding of these places a viable proposition until after Naseby, when the full force of the New Model Army and its formidable train of artillery reduced them, one by one, to ruins.

Hence throughout the Civil War we have Royalists who fought purely on a parochial basis against their neighbours, and some interesting amateur sieges resulted. All kinds of subterfuge were employed to make up for lack of ordnance, mines were used and even the medieval device of piling brushwood against a gate to burn it down was not scorned. As with castles and manors, so with towns, particularly those with their medieval walls intact. One wonders whether the good burghers were not more interested in the preservation of their goods than the service of the King. If so it was a short-sighted policy, for there were enough good men penned behind walls to replace the infantry lost at Naseby, and in war, as in chess, defensive play cannot win. The archaeologist can only condemn the policy of Parliament in 1644–5 of destroying strongholds, rather than garrisoning them, but militarily this procedure can only be commended, for it did not weaken the strength of the field army, and after all, wars are won in the field.

Thomas Venn gave this advice to the besieged: 'The first beginning is to keep the enemy from the town as far off and as long as you can. Therefore whatsoever without the works can put a stop to the enemy, the Besiegers [i.e. the besieged] must possess and defend as long as they can. They must use all their endeavour to hinder the approach of the enemy, therefore let them sally frequently, but warily, lest they fall into snares to the irreparable loss of the town.'[1] However, it is one thing to sketch out a set of rules in a council chamber and quite another to carry them out under active service conditions.

A good example is the siege of Basing House, which withstood three major assaults and a number of minor ones between July 1643 and October 1645. Irritated by a number of small probing attacks, John Paulet, fifth Marquis of Winchester, petitioned the King to put a garrison into Basing House, his ancestral home, in July 1643. It was an enormous place, part residence, part fortress, covering some $14\frac{1}{2}$ acres. The Old House, surrounded by a Norman earthwork, contained a miscellany of buildings, dating from the Saxon period onwards, and had been modernised by William Paulet who was Comptroller and Treasurer of the Household to Henry VIII. He had also built the 380-roomed New House adjoining it and surrounded both houses by a wall almost a mile round, 9 feet thick, of brick with a rammed earth core with towers at intervals. Its north front was also screened by the narrow marshy valley through which the river Loddon flows.

The first attack, led by Colonel Richard Norton (a local man, whose house was at Old Alresford) with a troop of horse and one of dragoons, coincided with the arrival of 100 musketeers from Oxford under Lieutenant-Colonel Robert Peake. Norton, not knowing of the garrison and thinking to secure an easy prey, was beaten off. The first major attack was mounted by Waller later that year. His force was composed of 16 troops of horse, 8 companies of dragoons, and 36 companies of foot, while his train of artillery was composed of 10 heavy cannon and 6 cases of small drakes. The garrison of the House, strengthened by a further 140 men under the aged Colonel Sir Marmaduke Rawdon, now numbered some 400 men. Sporadic attacks took place during the afternoon and evening, possibly to screen the siting of the guns on the rising ground north of the House known as Cowdray's Down. At daybreak on 7 November they opened fire across the valley.

Later that day an all out assault was launched against the north face. The Grange, a fortified farmhouse which partially covered the front, was taken, and the Roundhead musketeers now had cover and a rest for their weapons which no doubt improved their accuracy. A strange impromptu banquet took place as parties of the enemy feasted on the stores meant for the Royalist garrison, while others kept up the fight. There was little cover for the attackers on the north-east angle, however, for all the village cottages had been burnt, to deny them shelter. Enraged at the Roundhead feast, the garrison sent out a sortie which fired the barns and retired back into the House. The attack continued into the evening when a rainstorm compelled the Parliamentarian forces to retreat to their quarters. By reason of the weather, Waller withdrew his forces to billets in the surrounding villages and did not return to the attack until 12 November.

After a mutual bombardment, the Roundheads made an assault from all sides, 'giving a hot and desperate charge'.[2] Again it met a spirited defence in which even the ladies of the House took a part, and again the attackers were beaten off at

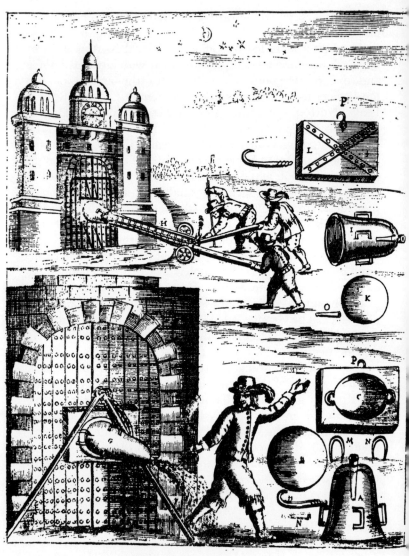

Methods of fixing a petard.
Malthus, Pratique de la Guerre (1631)

dusk. No doubt there would have been further assaults, but hearing of Lord Hopton's advance from Salisbury Waller prudently withdrew.

The second major attack was not launched until 11 July 1644, but it must not be supposed that the interim was a time of peace and quiet for Basing. With the local Roundhead headquarters only 20 miles away at Farnham, there were frequent sorties and skirmishes with varying results. The garrison also did a great deal of spade work, covering the exposed southern face with breastworks and bastions in preparation for the siege they knew must eventually come. The second attack, like the first, was led by Norton. He commanded a force of 2,000 men. Having observed the failure of Waller's method, he determined to starve the House into submission. Gradually the breastworks crept round the perimeter. Colonel Herbert Morley's pikemen and musketeers blanketed the southern approaches, Colonel Sir Richard Onslow's men on the right of Morley's covered the lower lane to Basingstoke and the close in between. Guards of horse continually patrolled between the close and the church, completing the circuit. This treatment was more to be feared than all Waller's assaults and in the House belts were soon tightened. Then such cannon and mortars as were available were sent to aid the besieging force. To the perils of famine were added the dangers of bombardment.

By September, conditions were so bad in the depleted garrison that Paulet sent a desperate message to the Cavalier headquarters at Oxford saying that unless a relief force was sent within ten days, he must surrender. At first the Governor of Oxford, Sir Arthur Aston, well aware of the dangers of the attempt, would have vetoed the request, but Colonel Henry Gage persuaded him to allow him to lead a picked relief force. By force and cunning he made his way through 40 miles of enemy infested territory, broke up the siege and, cutting his way through, revictualled the garrison, an exploit for which he received a knighthood. When he returned to Oxford, the noose drew tight around the House again. Within another two months the Roundhead breastworks were pushed closer and closer to the walls. However, with the King's stand-off victory at Second Newbury on 26 October, the balance of power in the district shifted once again.

Captured at Basing

When Sir Henry Gage, at the head of 1,000 troopers, again relieved the House on 20 November, he found that Norton had evacuated his lines the day before, after a siege of twenty-four weeks. The garrison was down to the barest necessities, the soldiers spent and threadbare. Besides wounded and deserters they had lost 100 men through action and sickness. Another period of uneasy quiet ensued. On 14 June 1645 came the fatal day of Naseby when the Royal army was shattered and the King's cause virtually lost. Parliament now had the time and the equipment to turn to the problem of reducing those stubborn places that still held out. The man they sent to deal with Basing was a Dutch engineer, Colonel John Dalbier, and arriving on 20 August he went about his work slowly and methodically. His trained mind looked over the structures, calculating how much leverage should be applied and where to bring about a dramatic collapse of the fabric with the least expenditure of material.

It took him a month to formulate his plans, site his guns and open fire. It was no random bombardment. On 22 September a great tower in the Old House collapsed, then the guns were turned on the New House. First bricks were loosened in the main fabric and a long sinuous crack appeared. Then the cannons were trained on the huge corner turret which came crashing down on 27 September, bringing with it a great slab of the wall and exposing the rooms. Dalbier's force at this time numbered 1,000 foot and 4 troops of horse. On 8 October Cromwell himself, fresh from the reduction of Winchester, arrived to finish the task. He wasted no time. Paulet was invited to surrender, and refused. The great siege guns in Cromwell's train opened fire on 12 October. One at least was the heaviest type of cannon then in use, firing a 63-pound shot, while two others fired a 27-pound shot. The General had brought with him a further 6,000 men. With no possibility of relief, the writing was on the wall, but the defenders, mostly Roman Catholics, were resolved to hold out. Within twenty-four hours the walls had been breached in at least two places and on 14 October, at six o'clock in the morning, the flood tide of the Roundhead army swept through the breaches, taking the place in two hours, despite a desperate defence by the depleted garrison, now reduced to 300 men, many of whom fell. The place was looted and burnt to the ground within twenty-four hours. 'A good encouragement', was Cromwell's comment.

It must not be concluded that this kind of diehard determination was peculiar to the male sex, or to the siege of Basing. The defence of Wardour Castle by Lady Arundel, of Corfe by Lady Bankes and of Lathom House[3] by the Countess of Derby lends support to Kipling's dictum that the female of the species is more deadly than the male. No doubt the Roundheads expected an easy victory and a speedy capitulation at Lathom, but the Countess, whose husband was absent

in the King's service, belonged to the warlike French family
of La Tremouille, and was a woman of high courage. On 27
February the Parliamentarian force investing the stronghold
consisted of some 2,500 men under 4 colonels, Ralph Ashton,
Holland, John Moore and Alexander Rigby. Their men were
divided into tertias so that there was always a watch set, each
body being on guard every third day. Their artillery consisted of 1 demi-cannon (24-pounder), 1 culverin (15-
pounder), 3 sakers (5¼-pounders) and 1 mortar. On 28
February Sir Thomas Fairfax proposed a conference at New
Park, a house about a quarter of a mile from Lathom.
The Countess's answer, obviously framed to gain time, was
couched in these terms: ' . . . notwithstanding her present
condition, she remembered her lord's honour and her own
birth, conceiving it must be more knightly that Sir Thomas
Fairfax should wait upon her than she on him.'

Messages went to and fro and fighting did not begin until
12 March. Meanwhile the Roundheads had not been idle but
had made lines of circumvallation about the house. 'Their
works were an open trench round the house, a yard of ditch
and a yard of raised turf at a distance sixty, one hundred, and
two hundred yards from the walls.' They raised eight sconces
where they thought they would be most useful to annoy the
Cavaliers in any sortie. These were built with 'two yards of
ditch, in some places staked and palisaded to keep off a violent
assault'. To protect their pioneers while digging their trenches,
approaches and saps they used baskets and hurdles in the
usual way and also brought up a kind of testudo, or
wooden engine running on wheels, roofed towards the
house with thick planks and open for the enemy to cast up
earth.

The Countess's resources were slender. She had not a single
field officer, but her six captains were William Farmer (killed
at Marston Moor), a Scottish professional soldier, William
Farrington, Charnock, Edward Chisenhall, Edward Rosethorne and Molineux Radcliffe. Lieutenant William Key
commanded 12 horse and there were 300 foot organised in 6
companies of 50. The ordnance consisted of 6 sakers and 2

sling pieces. In the walls there were 7 towers sited to flank each other. These towers were manned during the hours of daylight by 16 selected marksmen and also contained one or two 'murderers' to scour the ditches. Outside the walls was a deep ditch fenced on each bank with strong palisades. There was a severe shortage of powder but the captains 'dispensed it frugally and prohibited the soldiers from waste of shots'. Besides that captured from the enemy in sorties only 7 barrels were spent during the whole siege. The Countess husbanded her provisions with equal frugality. When relief eventually came there still remained sufficient for two months.

The first sortie was led by Captain Farmer, 'a faithful and gallant soldier', and Lieutenant Bretergh, 'ready to second him in any service'. The party consisted of 100 foot and the 12 horse. Farmer, 'determined to do something that might remind the enemy that there were soldiers within, boldly marched right up to the works without a shot and they firing upon them in their trenches swiftly persuaded them to leave their holes.' Lieutenant Key, sallying from another gate, fell upon the fleeing Roundheads with much execution. In this well managed affair the besiegers lost 30 men, 40 arms, a drum and six prisoners. The garrison lost not a single man.

The bombardment commenced on 20 March, when the Roundheads fired four shots from the big 24-pounder: ' . . . they first tried the walls . . . being found proof, without yielding or showing the least impression; they afterward shot higher to beat down the pinnacles and turrets.' The same day Sir Thomas Fairfax again tried to dissuade the Countess from continuing the struggle by means of a letter from the Earl of Derby who desired a safe conduct for his wife. The lady's reply was, as usual, spirited. 'She would willingly submit herself to her lord's commands and therefore wishes the general to treat with him; but until she was assured that such was his lordship's pleasure, she would neither yield up the house, nor desert it herself, but await for the event according to the good will of God.' She also managed to convey this message to her

husband where he lay at Chester, getting the bearer through
the besiegers' lines by a stratagem. Four days passed without
more than alarums and excursions, then on 25 March the
besiegers sent over seven shots from their heavy guns, one of
which crashed through the great gates which were immediately barricaded. From then on a daily bombardment became
commonplace. On 1 April they fired chain-shot and bars of
iron and the next day they brought into action the mortar
that Rigby had borrowed from Sir William Brereton. It fired
three times, hurling stones measuring 13 inches and weighing
80 lb. This mortar was 'planted about half a musket shot,
south-west from the house, on rising ground conveniently
giving the engineer a full prospect of the whole building'. It
was sited in a moon-shaped work with $2\frac{1}{2}$ yards of turf above
the ditch. On 4 April this mortar again sent over a grenado
and a stone which soared right over the house.

By 10 April the garrison no doubt felt that they had
suffered enough of this treatment and decided to retaliate.
Once more they sallied out. Issuing from a postern with a
force composed of half the garrison, Captain Farmer, seconded by Lieutenants Penketh and Worrill, beat the rebels from
all their works and batteries, spiked the cannons, took sixty
arms, a set of colours and three drums. The Roundheads
seemed quite demoralised by these *blitzkreig* tactics, for
instead of withdrawing hastily to the sally port the Royalists
marched back through the great gates which Captain Ogle
was guarding with a party of musketeers. Covering fire was
provided by Captain Rosethorne, who placed his musketeers
to advantage on the walls.

All this was normal practice, though one device at least
may have been original: 'Captain Fox with colours in the
Eagle Tower gave signals when to march and when to retreat,
according to the motions of the enemy, which he observed at
a distance.' The Roundhead gunners must have known their
trade, for despite the nailing of the guns, they were able to
reopen fire again that night and on 12 April managed to put a
saker ball through a window in Lady Derby's chamber. On
the 15th the mortar spoke again, firing five times with stones

and once with a grenado that fell short, though pieces of the shell, 2 inches thick, flew over the walls and were taken up into the furthest part of the house (similar pieces may be seen to this day in Lichfield Cathedral). This weapon was the one thing that troubled the garrison. Morale was raised when a Roundhead engineer, 'mounting the rampart to see the fall of the grenado', was picked off by one of the marksmen stationed in the tower. On 20 April the Roundheads fired thirty shots from their demi-cannon and culverin, battering a postern tower with little effect. On Easter Monday (22 April) the bombardment was stepped up with nine cannons opening fire. The garrison was of the opinion that this was for propaganda purposes, to amuse the country people who had come to watch the siege. Next day the big guns fired twenty-three times. Halsall suggests that this was because of the second wake (an annual holiday), and that Rigby 'must gratify the country for their £2,000* by the battery of the Eagle Tower'. Two shots entered Lady Derby's chamber compelling her at last to seek a new lodging.

On 25 April Rigby sent a surrender demand by a drummer. Tearing the paper into fragments the Countess said grimly, 'A due reward for thy pains would be to hang thee at my gate. But thou art only the foolish instrument of a traitor's pride; carry this answer back to Rigby', and playing for effect before her soldiers, who witnessed the whole scene, she delivered a brief but telling harangue assuring him that rather than fall into Rigby's hands she and her children would die in the flames of Lathom House. It had the desired effect on the soldiers. 'We will die for his majesty and your honour', they shouted. 'God save the King!' As soon as the messenger departed the Countess and her captains held a Council of War. 'The mortar piece was that which troubled us all. The little ladies had stomach to digest cannon, but the stoutest soldiers had no heart for grenadoes.' After a long debate it was resolved that though there was a battery covering every sally port they would issue out the next morning 'and venture all'. The officers' tasks were apportioned thus:

* Presumably the assessment.

Captain Edward Chisenhall	
Captain Richard Fox	
Lieutenant Bretergh	
Lieutenant Penket	Sortie
Lieutenant Walthen	
Lieutenant Worrill	
Captain Henry Ogle	Main guard. To secure retreat through the southern gate.
Captain Edward Rosethorne	Sally gate on east side to secure retreat.
Captain Molineux Radcliffe	Marksmen and musketeers on wall.
Captain William Farmer	Reserve of fresh men on the parade.

Chisenhall with eighty men sallied out of the east gate and after a skirmish entered the fort where the Roundheads had planted their great guns, slaying many and taking some prisoner. The rest fled. Fox now seconded Chisenhall, beating up the trenches from the eastern to the south-western corner where the mortar was. It was guarded by fifty men and the work surrounding it was so high that the musketeers had no target but had to beat the enemy out with stones. The offshot of this whole daring attack was that they captured the mortar and, lifting it by sheer strength onto a rough sledge, dragged it back in triumph to the House. The sortie lasted barely an hour and the garrison lost only two men mortally wounded. The worst was now over. With the mortar gone the Roundheads tried mining but heavy rain made their tunnel collapse. On 23 May, Rigby and Holland again summoned the Countess to surrender, and to submit to the mercy of Parliament. '. . . the mercies of the wicked are cruel,' was her comment. Once more the soldiers heard her reject the summons with acclamation. Their ordeal was almost at an end. That very night, a messenger slipped into the House to report that Prince Rupert and the Earl of Derby, having stormed Bolton, were marching to their relief. On the night of 25–26 May, Rigby lifted the siege and stole away. On 29 May Sir Richard Crane, the commander of Rupert's Lifeguard, entered Lathom in triumph and presented the Countess with the colours captured in the Prince's latest victory as trophies and a tribute to her valour.

During the siege it was estimated that the Roundhead casualties were about 500 killed and another 140 wounded. These figures seem rather high. They had fired 107 cannon balls and 32 stones, and had sent 4 grenadoes (shells) into the House, besides expending nearly 100 barrels of powder. The Royalists admitted only 6 killed, while the number of their wounded is not known. Although the Royalist chroniclers' statistics may be suspect, it had been a determined and brilliant defence.

These two sieges have been chosen as typical, but there were many more too numerous to mention, particularly during the last part of the war when the King's cause was declining and his followers, although no longer masters of the field, were determined to fight on. Equally stirring accounts could be written of the defence of the castles of Pontefract, Harlech, Farringdon and Donnington, Greenland House and so on *ad infinitum*. From the evidence a general pattern of attack may be deduced:

1. Reconnaissance. Selection of points of attack. Opening of trenches, siting of guns. Summons to surrender.
2. Circumvallation.
3. Commence approaches. Bombardment.
4. Breaching of walls by mine or cannon.
5. Intaking by storm—or relief.

TERMS OF SURRENDER

So far we have seen sieges where the assailants or the defenders were violently successful. Sometimes it was necessary to come to terms with the enemy, either because the stronghold had been reduced to indefensible rubble – as at Greenland House – or because of the faintheartedness of the defenders, as at Farnham Castle and Bletchingdon House. The surrender of Winchester Castle by Lord Ogle seems to fall between these two categories. After Naseby, as we have seen, Fairfax turned

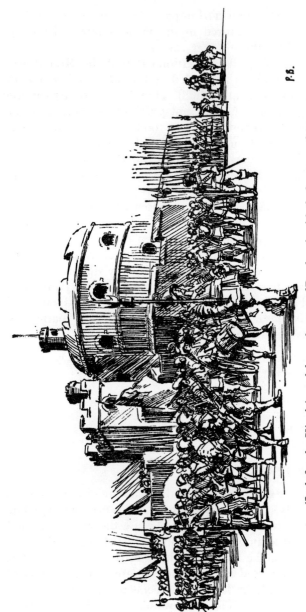

'Jack-for-the-King' Arundel marches out of Pendennis with the honours of war

P.B.

his attention and the strength of the New Model Army to reducing such southern strongholds as still held out for the King. Winchester Castle, which appears on Speed's map as having two wards and many towers, was constructed adjacent to the west gate of the city. Milner tells us that it was about 850 feet north to south, while from west to east it was 250 feet.[4] The keep was about 100 feet square and connected by a wall to the southern defences of the city. It was flanked by four towers, one at each corner, and another at the entrance facing north. The main gate faced west, on the other side of the ditch was a strong barbican in which a guard was posted. Square towers looked down into the moat which varied in depth but was said to be 100 feet deep near the keep. A mighty stronghold it must have been in medieval times, but its founder, William I, had no conception of the power of the Parliamentarian guns 500 years later. Cromwell wrote: 'I summoned the Castle and was denied, whereupon we fell to preparing our batteries which we could not perfect until Friday morning [4 October 1645]. Our battery was six guns which being finished, after firing one round I sent in a second summons for treaty which was refused.'[5] However, the Roundhead guns had not battered long at the castle when the noble lord had a change of heart, and hauling down his red flag of defiance began to treat for surrender; then, strangely enough, he again changed his mind and broke off the negotiations. It was said that other officers of his garrison persuaded him of the possibility of relief with this result. The bombardment that followed was continuous and heavy. According to Cromwell 200 shots were fired, with the result that a breach 'wide enough to march 30 men through was made'[6] by the Sunday night. Preparations were made to storm it at first light next morning, but at 10 o'clock in the evening Ogle beat a parley desiring to treat in these terms:

Sir – I have received formerly a letter from you wherein you desire to avoid the effusion of Christian blood to which you received my answer that I was as willing as yourself. But having had no reply [to advance] your desires I have thought fit to desire a treaty whereby we might pitch up some means both for the effecting of that and the preservation of this place. And that I may receive your letter with all convenience I desire that neither officer or soldier of your party may come off their guards and I shall take a like course with mine.

Your humble servant   Ogle.
Winton Castle at eight at night
October 5 1645.

Colonel Hammond and Major Harrison, soon to figure largely in the storm of Basing House, were detached as the Parliament's emissaries and spent most of the night in discussion of terms. By daylight they had hammered out a formula for the surrender as follows:[7]

1. Ogle was to deliver up the castle with all its ordnance, arms and ammunition without embezzlement, waste or spoil.
2. Ogle and his officers should march forth with their side arms only.
3. Ogle should march out with his own company with colours flying and drums beating.
4. He should have 100 fixed arms for his guard and 100 men to guard them as far as Woodstock. Hostages were to be given for the safety of this convoy.
5. All the common soldiers should stack their arms and disperse.
6. Ogle and his officers should have safe conveyance with their horses, arms and goods as far as Woodstock, six carriages (carts) being allowed for this purpose.

Much argument went on afterwards that Ogle had not pressed the defence as vigorously as he might, but he was exonerated at a court martial held at the Governor's lodging at Oxford on 12 November 1645. That such an occasion was regarded as a great spectacle amongst the civilian population is shown from Wood's revelation that 'on 10 June 1646 the garrison of Boarstall was surrendered for the use of Parliament.'[8] The schoolboys were let out by their master that day

Wood and his schoolfellows watch the wounded Colonel Blagge being chased back to Wallingford Castle

and many of them trudged the four miles from Thame to Boarstall, arriving between 8 and 9 o'clock in the morning, 'to see the forme of surrender, the strength of the garrison, and the soldiers of each partie'. Wood was told not to taste any provisions belonging to the garrison lest the Royalists should have poisoned them! In any case he found that he could not get in, 'but stood, as hundreds did, without the works where he saw the Governor, Sir William Campion, a little man, who upon some occasion or other laid flat on his belly to write a letter or bill, or the form of a pass, or some such thing'.[9] If they had a holiday every time a Royalist garrison surrendered in those woeful months following Naseby, then indeed their schooling must have suffered.

REFERENCES

1. Venn, Book 2, 'Exact Method of . . . Fortifying Towns . . . and Defending Same', 1672.
2. Archer.
3. References to the siege of Lathom House are found in Lancashire Civil War Tracts, Chetham Society 1844.
4. Dr Milner's *History of Winchester*, vol. ii, shows an engraving of two faces of the castle.
5. Cromwell's report to Sir Thomas Fairfax.
6. ibid.
7. ibid.
8. Wood 1 p. 127.
9. ibid. 1 p. 128.

Chapter Thirteen

Aftermath

Honest men served you faithfully in this action. Sir, they are trusty,
I beseech you in the name of God not to discourage them.
He that ventures his life for the liberty of his country,
I wish he trust God for the liberty of his conscience
and you for the liberty he fights for.

Oliver Cromwell after Naseby

The narrative of a book, whether it is fact or fiction, is sealed
between its covers. The reader enters the lives of the characters
at a certain stage and leaves them somewhat further on—
whether years, months or days later depends on the scope of
the book. If the story has been well told, the reader may
wonder what happened to the characters afterwards, beyond
the last full stop and the back cover. It is with this question
that this chapter is concerned.

Once the last spark of armed Royalist resistance had been
quenched there was nothing for the ordinary Cavalier soldier
to do but go home. After the first rapturous welcome from his
family and friends, his natural joy at being home, and the
relief of knowing that he need no longer sleep on the ground
with his weapons at hand, or forage for his food, he may have
felt, as he tried to pick up the threads of his ordinary civilian
life, how indescribably dull and safe it was. Although it may
be the soldier's greatest desire to get out of uniform and away
from hardship, discipline and bloodshed, to his astonishment
and dismay he finds coming out as big a break as going in.
One misses the uncertainty, the excitement and above all the
comradeship; it is quite a psychological contradiction. However, our seventeenth-century Thomas Atkins, if he was wise,
worked hard at being a civilian again and, in time, found that

he had slipped back into his little groove, even if he was never quite the same human being again. He never could be after such experiences as Edgehill, Marston Moor and Naseby. Some probably came back dishonest, brutal and drunken, others mature, more tolerant and enlightened, but none escaped unmarked. There must have been many who found themselves unable to settle down and took ship to the Continent as mercenaries, perhaps never to be seen again. Many wives never saw their husbands again and never knew what became of them. There was no army records office then; no telegram from the War Office. The plight of these women is summed up in a poignant letter addressed to a husband in one of the regiments attacking Basing House:

Most deare and loving husband, my king love, I remember unto you hoping you are in good health as I ame at the writting therof. My little Willie have bene sick this fortnight. I pray you to come whome if youe cane cum saffly. I doo marfull that I cannot heere from you ass well other naybores do. I do desiere to heer from you as soon as you cane. I pray you to send me word when youe thenke youe shoude returne. Youe doe not consider I ame a lone woemane, I thought youe woald never leave me thuse long togeder, so I rest evere praying for your savese returne
your loving wife
Susan Rodway.
Ever praying for you till deth I depart. To my very loving husbane Robert Rodway a traine soudare in the Red Regiment under the command of Captain Warrene. Deliver this with all Spide.

Unlike the men of the 'regular' regiments who went wherever the war took them, these trained bands were meant for purely parochial defence and were 'lent out' on a limited time basis. In this case, as we know, Susan was not left long in suspense, for the Westminster (Red) Regiment was home for Christmas. The continued silence of the husband has an ominous ring, however, for Captain Warren led a 'forlorn hope' attack against the walls of Basing House with loss. Could it be that

Robert Rodway was even then in a soldier's grave? We can never know. This is all that may be conjectured about the aftermath as it affected the common man. He sank back into the anonymity from which he emerged to fight for his beliefs, and little more is heard from him except in instances where he applies for relief in conditions of hardship.

If the fate of these men was obscure, however, the future of many of the officers is well documented. Many survived to the Restoration in 1660 and claimed their share of the £60,000 granted by Charles II 'for the relief of his Truly Loyal and Indigent Party'. Of course, many had been promoted and had served other colonels since 1642. They included:

		Listed under	*Rank and Regt in 1642 if different*
Stafford	Capt. Robt Fleetwood	Beaumont F	
	Capt. Anthony Dormer		
L & W	Capt. Will Wolverston	Belasyse F	
Lincoln	Capt. Thos Booth		
L & W	Lt.-Colonel Sir Bartholomew Pell	Sir Theophilus Gilby F	Capt. Belasyse
Stafford	Q.M. Hugh Grainger	Earl of Bristol	Digby H
		Col. John Lane	
Lincoln	Capt. Martin Frobisher		Subaltern
Lincoln	Capt. Thos. Cardinall	Dutton F	Lieut. ?
L & W	Capt. Thos Hull		
Berks	Lieut. Sam Hull		
Kent	Capt. Geo Grimes		Lieut.
	Major Charles Kirk	Hawkins F	Captain, Dutton F
	Ensign Ed. Jordon		
Bedford	Ensign John Halley	Fielding F	
L & W	Major Chas. Norwood	*do.*	
Hereford	Lt.-Col. Thos. Coningby	Lord Astley F	Capt.
L & W	Lieut. Francis Bowles	*do.*	Lieut.
L & W	Lt.-Col. Urian Leigh	Fitton F	Major
Chester	Capt. Peter Leigh	Thelwall F	
Chester	Capt. Charles Leigh	*do.*	
Montgom.	Cornet Meredith Floyd	Lord Grandison H	
Northum.	Lieut. Edmond Roddam	Grey D.	

		Listed under	Rank and Regt in *1642* if different
Wilts.	Q.M. Thos. Rutter	Lord Bernard Stuart Lifeguard H	
L & W	Lt.-Col. Sir Wm. Leighton	Earl of Lindsey Lifeguard F.	Major

The list, of course, goes on at some length; this is merely an extract. A relatively small number of Royalist officers found employment in the post-Restoration army of King Charles II, but the establishment was so small that many were glad enough to serve in the ranks. Captain John Gwyn, for example, served as a trooper in the Lifeguard, and Lieutenant Robert Wright trailed a pike, under Colonel John Russell, in the regiment that is now the Grenadier Guards.

Pensioners of 1660

After every war there are limbless and blind ex-soldiers in most towns. In the time of Elizabeth I the state began to realise that it had a certain responsibility for the welfare of such people, and a statute was passed enacting that parishes could be rated for the support of maimed soldiers and mariners. An applicant for a pension was required to produce a certificate from the officer under whom he had served or the respectable inhabitants of his parish. In addition to the granting of pensions the Justices could order the church wardens to give parish relief to help the families of distressed soldiers. It would seem that there existed a subtle difference between volunteers and conscripts: the latter were relieved as paupers might be, while pensions were granted to the former. One such application reads:

> We are informed that Thomas Scaife first took up arms when H.M. set up his standard at Nottingham and was in his Highness the Prince's troops, now King of England, and was wounded at Edgehill fight and died in the service of Charles I . . . never revolted and hath left Janie Scaife his child an orphant who hath not wherewith to mayntayne herself . . . We the J.P.s of Yorks. . . . think a pension should be given for her support. 20 August 1662.
> To William Hammond Esq. Treasurer for lame soldiers . . .
> [Signed] John Goodricke, Miles Stapilton, Will Fairfax

Some soldiers' needs were more immediate, and one Captain Euble Floyd petitioned the King at Oxford on 2 June 1644. He had seen service since the beginning of the rebellion in 1642, had served as Lieutenant and Captain-Lieutenant in Colonel Charles Gerrard's regiment of foot, and at Alresford was smitten with a musket shot 'in the midst of the back. Still lies in pain. Has only received ½ week's pay, cost of physicians etc. is great, dependent on friends. His arrears of pay are great. Prays relief.' The action taken was to grant him £20, not a great sum nowadays possibly, but then worth perhaps £200. Other deserving cases included 'Jasper Edmond, a soldier under Captain Floyd of Colonel Garret's [Gerrard] regiment who came out of Montgomery and was at Edgehill shot in the knee and lost the whole limb'; 'John Oakes, organist of Gloucester Cathedral fled the city and joined Colonel Windham prays for place in Wells Cathedral'; 'Thomas Pritchard, a poor maimed soldier under Cap. Hopkins, shot in the leg at Edgehill, can't use it, prays for almsman's place at Christchurch, Off'. And so they went on and on. The price that must be paid for military glory and victory. A list of pensions granted in the Nottinghamshire Quarter Sessions Minute Book reads:

9th January 1654

George Gray	£2	Alice Gale Widdoe	£1
Nicholas Worthing	£1	Mary Hoe *do.*	£2
Richard Grampton	£3	Elizabeth Morse	£2
Eliz. Butler widdoe	£3	Anthony Crossland	£1
Christopher Bassey	£4	Eliz. Wilsmore widoe	£2
Thos. Lynne orphant	£2	Eliz. Brerely widow	£1
Eliz. Okeland widow	£2	Helen Walker	£2

When Charles II came to the throne he was assailed by petitions for the recovery of debts incurred by his father in the prosecution of the war. To quote only two of them:

William Gary of Bushmead, Beds, Commissioned Captain of Horse Co. Huntingdonshire and commanded at own cost and charge. Attended Charles I to Scotland. Helped carry plate from Cambridge [there follows a list of his services to the King]. Went to Colchester siege, captured and sent to Lincoln as prisoner, lost £1,200 in all.

[Signed]   Cleveland Thos. Wentworth   Bruce
                John Russell   Hen' Capell

And Captain Phillip Ellis, Rose Castle, Cumberland:

At our own charge raised company of foot and troop of horse as Captain-Lieutenant by several commissions from the Earl of Newcastle. Continued without pay or free quarter for 4 years until the siege of Carlisle – supplied garrisons with provisions to value of £300 and more. Family subjected to much oppression. In 1648 commanded by

Langdale to secure Rose Castle and did so, kept it until stormed and burnt. Losses in all £3,000.

[Signed]	Phillip Musgrave	Thomas Dacre
	Edward Musgrave	William Huddleston
	John Lamplugh	Launcelot Walker
	James Patrickson	

The signatures were, of course, of those gentlemen who attested the truth of the statements in the petition. It is a hoary myth that King Charles II neglected the old Cavaliers. In fact practically all the officers of his small standing army had served in the Civil Wars, or were the sons of old Royalists. The £60,000 allotted to the indigent officers was a great sum for a seventeenth-century government. While there are injustices there will always be men who will risk all for what they believe to be right. To echo the inscription on the present bridge at Cropredy: 'From Civil War Good Lord Deliver us.'

Bibliography

Books mentioned by a single name in the References are here given in full.

Archer: *The Marching of the Red Trained Bands* . . . , Lieutenant Elias Archer 1643.

Atkyns/Gwyn: *The Vindication of Richard Atkyns* and *The Military Memoirs of John Gwyn*, edited by Peter Young and Norman Tucker in a single volume (Longmans).

Bariffe: *Military Discipline or the Young Artilleryman*, William Bariffe, 2nd edition 1639.

Bulstrode: *Memoirs and Reflections*, Sir Richard Bulstrode, published 1721.

Davies: *The Parliamentary Army under the Earl of Essex 1642–5*, Godfrey Davies, 1934.

Clarendon: *The History of the Rebellion and Civil Wars in England*, Edward, Earl of Clarendon. Commenced in 1641. The 1888 edition (W. Dunn Macray, Oxford University Press), used throughout.

Emberton: *Love Loyalty: The Story of the Close and Perilous Siege of Basing House 1643–5*, Wilf Emberton, 1972.

Fasnacht/Blackwell: *A History of the City of Oxford*, Ruth Fasnacht, Basil Blackwell (Blackwell 1954).

Firth: *Cromwell's Army*, C. H. Firth, 4th edition (Methuen 1962).

Grose: *Military Antiquities*, F. Grose.

Hamilton: *The Duties of a Regimental Surgeon* . . . , Robert Hamilton MD, 1794.

Ludlow: *Memoirs of Edmund Ludlow*, edited by C. H. Firth, 1894.

Monck: *Observations upon Political and Military Affairs*, 1671, Colonel George Monck, later 1st Duke of Albemarle.

Peacock: *The Army Lists of the Roundheads and Cavaliers . . . 1642*, edited by Edward Peacock, 2nd edition 1874.

Prince Rupert's Diary: these notes are preserved in the Wiltshire Records Office at Trowbridge.

Roy: *The Royalist Ordnance Papers 1642–6*, Part 1, Dr Ian Roy (Oxfordshire Record Society 1964).

Rushworth: *Historical Collections* . . . *1618–1701*, John Rushworth, 7 volumes, 1659–1701.

Venn: *Military Observation or the Tacticks Put into Practice*, Captain Thomas Venn, 1672.

Warburton: *Memoirs of Prince Rupert and the Cavaliers*, Eliot Warburton, 1849.

Wharton: *Letters by Sergeant Nehemiah Wharton* . . . , edited by Sir Henry Ellis. *Archaeologia* vol. 25, 1853, p. 313.

Winstock: *Songs and Marches of the Roundheads and Cavaliers*, Lewis S. Winstock, 1972. Also the record *Songs and Music of the Redcoats 1642–1902*, Argo ZDA 147.

Wood: *Wood's Life and Times* and *Wood's City of Oxford*, collected from the diaries and other papers of Anthony Wood, antiquary at Oxford 1632–95, by Andrew Clark MA (Oxford Historical Society 1891).

Young: *Edgehill* and *Marston Moor*, Brigadier Peter Young DSO, MC, MA (Roundwood Press 1967).

Life of James II . . . *collected out of Memoirs writ of his own hand*, edited by T. S. Clarke, 1816. (For Edgehill see pp. 9–18.)

Lawes and Ordinances of Warre (1642)

(Godwin Pamphlets vol. 117, 14, reproduced by courtesy of the curators of the Bodleian Library)

OF DUTIES TO GOD

1

Blasphemy   First, let no man presume to blaspheme the holy and blessed Trinity, God the Father, God the Son, and God the Holy Ghost; nor the known Articles of our Christian Faith, upon pain to have his Tongue bored with a red-hot iron.

2

Cursing   Unlawful Oaths and Execrations, and scandalous acts in derogation of God's Honour, shall be punished with loss of Pay, and other punishment at discretion.

3

Neglecting Divine Worship   All those who often and wilfully absent themselves from Sermons, and Public Prayer, shall be proceeded against at discretion: and all such who shall violate the Places of Public worship, shall undergo severe Censure.

OF DUTIES IN GENERAL

1

Intelligence with the Enemy   All such as shall practice and entertain Intelligence with the enemy, by any manner or means or slights, and have any communication with them, without direction from the Lord Generall, shall be punished as Traitors and Rebels.

2

Relief of the Enemy   No man shall relieve the Enemy, with money, victuals, ammunition, neither harbour or receive such, upon pain of death.

3

Yielding Up of Forts If a town, castle, or fort be yielded up without the utmost necessity, the Governor thereof shall be punished with death.

4

But if so it be, that the Officers and Souldiers of the Garrison constrain the Governor to yield it up; in such a case shall all the Officers be punished with death, and the Common soldiers who have been active or have given their consent in constraining the Governor, shall cast lots for the hanging of the 10th man amongst them.

5

And withall to know in what case and circumstances a Governor, and the militia of the Garrison may be blameless, for the surrendering of a town, castle or fort, it is hereby expressly signified: that first they are to prove extremity of want within the place, insomuch that no eatable provision was left them for the sustenance of their lives. Secondly, that no succour or relief in any probable wise could be hoped for. Thirdly, that nothing else could be expected, but that within a short time the town, castle or fort with all the garrison and arms, ammunition, magazine and appurtenances in it, must of necessity, fall into the hands of the enemy. Upon proof of which forementioned circumstances, they may be acquainted in a Counsel of War, else to be liable to the punishment above expressed.

6

Careless Service Whosoever shall be convicted to do his duty negligently and carelessly, shall be punished at discretion.

7

Violating of a Safe-Guard Whosoever shall presume to violate a Safe-guard, shall die without mercy.

8

Whosoever shall come from the enemy, without a trumpet or drum, after the custom of war, or without a pass from His Excellence within the quarters of the army, or within a garrison town, shall be hanged up as a spy.

OF DUTIES TOWARDS SUPERIORS
AND COMMANDERS

I

Violating the Lord General   Whosoever shall use any words tending to the death of the Lord Generall, shall be punished with death.

2

Quarrelling with Officers   No man shall presume to quarrell with his superior officer, upon pain of cashiering, and arbitrary punishment, nor to strike any such, upon pain of death.

3

Departing from Captains and Masters   No soldier shall depart from his captain, nor servant from his master, with licence, though he serve still in the Army, upon pain of death.

4

Silence in the Army   Every private soldier or man, upon pain of imprisonment shall keep silence when the Army is to take Lodging, or when it is marching, or Imbattalio, so as the Officers may be heard, and their Commandments executed.

5

Resisting against Correction   No man shall resist draw, lift, or offer to draw, or lift his weapon against any officer, correcting him orderly for his offence, upon pain of death.

6

Unlawful Assemblies   No person shall make any mutinous assemblies, or be present or assisting thereunto, or in, or by them, demand their pay, upon pain of death.

7

Resisting of the Provost Marshall   No man shall resist the Provost Marshall, or any other officer, in the execution of his Office, or break prison, upon pain of death.

8

Seditious Words   None shall utter any words of sedition and uproar, or mutiny, upon pain of death.

9

Concealing Mutinous Speeches   A heavy punishment shall be inflicted upon them, who after they have heard mutinous speeches, acquaint not their commanders with them.

10

Receiving of Injuries   Whosoever shall receive any injury and shall take his own satisfaction, shall be punished by imprisonment, and as it shall be thought fit by the Marshal-Court; but he that is injured shall be bound, if he do not forgive the injury, to seek reparation by complaint to his captain, or colonel, or other superior officer, and it shall be given him in ample manner.

OF DUTIES MORALE

1

Drunkenness   Drunkenness in an officer shall be punished with loss of place; in a common soldier, with such penalties as a court-marshal think fit.

2

Unnatural Abuses   Rapes, Ravishments, unnatural abuses shall be punished with death.

3

Adultry   Adultry, Fornication, and other dissolute lasciviousness, shall be punished with discretion, according to the quality of the offence.

4

Theft   Theft, and Robbery, exceeding the value of twelve pence shall be punished with death.

5

Provocation   No man shall use reproachful, nor provoking words, or act to any upon pain of imprisonment, and further punishment as shall be thought fit to be inflicted upon enemies to Discipline and service.

6

Seizing Upon Dead Mens Goods   No man shall take or spoil the goods of him that dyeth, or is killed in service, upon pain of restoring double the value, and arbitrary punishment.

7
Murder   Murder shall be expiated with the death of the murderer.

OF A SOLDIER'S DUTY TOUCHING HIS ARMS

1
Full Armour   All soldiers coming to their colours to watch or to be exercised shall come fully armed, upon pain of severe correction.

2
Slovenly Armour   None shall presume to appear with their armes unfixt, or indecently kept, upon pain of Arbitrary correction.

3
Loosing of Horses and Armes   If a trooper shall lose his horse or Hackney, or a foot-man any part of his armes, by negligence or lewdness, by dice or card he or they shall remain in quality of Pioners, and Scavengers, till they be furnished with as good as were lost, at their own charge.

4
Pawning or Selling of Armour   No soldier shall give to pawn, or sell his armour, upon pain of imprisonment, and punishment at discretion; and wheresoever any armour shall be found so sold or pawned, they shall be brought again into the army.

5
Wilful Spoiling of Horses   If a trooper shall spoil his horse willingly, of purpose to be rid of the service, he shall lose his horse, and remain in the camp for a pioner.

6
Borrowed Arms   If one borrows arms of another to pass the muster withall, the borrower shall be rigorously punished, and the lender shall forfeit his goods.

7
Embezzling of Ammunition   None shall presume to spoil, sell or carry away any ammunition delivered unto him, upon pain of death.

OF DUTY IN MARCHING

1

Waste and Extortion   None in their march through the Countries shall waste, spoil or extort any victuals, Money or pawn, from any subject, upon any pretence of want whatsoever, upon pain of death.

2

Taking of Horses out of the Plow   No soldier shall presume upon no occasion whatsoever, to take a Horse out of the plouw, or to wrong the Husbandmen in their person or cattle, or goods, upon pain of death.

3

Straggling from the Colours   No soldier, either Horse or Foot, shall presume in marching to straggle from his Troop or Company, or to march out of his rank, upon pain of death.

4

Spoiling of Trees   No soldier shall presume, in marching or lodging, to cut down any fruit-trees, or to deface, or spoil walks of trees, upon pain of severe punishment.

OF DUTIES IN THE CAMP AND GARRISON

1

Swerving from the Camp   No man shall depart a mile out of the Army or Camp without licence, upon pain of death.

2

Going In or Out by Wayes   No man shall enter, or go out of the Army, but by ordinary wayes, upon pain of death.

3

Drawing of Swords after Setting the Watch   No man shall presume to draw his sword without Order, after the watch is set, upon pain of death.

4

Giving a False Alarm   No man shall give a false alarm or discharge a piece in the night, or make any noise without lawful cause, upon pain of death.

5

Drawing Swords in a Quarrell　No man shall draw any Sword in a private quarrell within the camp, upon pain of death.

6

Revealing the Watchword　He that makes known the Watchword without order, or gives any other word but what is given by the Officers, shall die for it.

7

Offering Violence to Victuallers　No man shall do violence to any that bring Victuals to the Camp, upon pain of death.

8

Speaking with the Enemy's Messengers　None shall speak with a drum or trumpet, or any other sent by the enemy, without order, upon pain of punishment at discretion.

9

A Sentinel Asleep or Drunk　A Sentinel or Perdue found asleep, or drunk or foresaking their place before they be drawn off shall die for the offence without mercy.

10

Failing at the Rendevous　No man shall fail wilfully to come to the rendevous or garrison appointed him by the Lord General, upon pain of death.

11

Remaining Unenrolled in the Army　No man that carrieth arms, and pretends to be a soldier, shall remain three days in the Army without being enrolled in some company, upon pain of death.

12

Departing without Leave　No man that is enrolled shall depart from the Army, or garrison, or from his Colours, without Licence, upon pain of death.

13

Outstaying a Pass　No private soldier shall outstay his pass, without a certificate of the occasion, under the hand of a Magistrate at the next Muster, upon pain of losing his pay, during all the time of his absence.

14
Absenting from the Watch He that absents himself when the sign is given to set the watch, shall be punished at discretion, either with bread and water in prison, or with the Wooden Horse.

15
Discontented with their Quarters Whosoever shall express his discontent with his quarters given him in the camp, or garrison, shall be punished as a Mutineer.

16
Lying or Supping out of Quarters No officer, of what quality soever, shall go out of the quarter to dinner or supper, or lye out all night, without making his superior officer acquainted, upon pain of cashiering.

17
Keeping of the Quarters Clean All officers whose charge it is, shall see the quarters kept clean and sweet, upon pain of severe punishment.

18
Letting of Horses Feed in Sown Ground None shall presume to let their horses feed in sown ground whatsoever, or to endamage the husbandmen any way, upon severest punishment.

19
Whosoever shall in his quarter, abuse, beat, fright his landlord, or any person else in the family, or shall extort money or victuals, by violence from them, shall be proceeded against as a mutineer, and an enemy to discipline.

OF DUTIES IN ACTION
1
Repairing to the Colours upon an Alarm No man shall fail immediately to repair unto his Colours (except he be impotent by Lameness or Sickness) when an alarm is given, upon pain of death.

2
Flying No man shall abandon his colours, or fly away in Battle, upon pain of death.

3

Flinging Away Arms   If a Pike-man throw away his pike, or a Musketeer his musket or Bandileer, he or they shall be punished with death.

4

Burning and Wasting   No man shall burn any house, or barn be it of friend or foe, or wilfully spoil any corn, hay, or straw, or stacks in the fields, or any ship, boat, carriage or anything that may serve for the provision of the army without order, upon pain of death.

5

Killing an Enemy who Yields   None shall kill an enemy who yields, and throws down his arms.

6

Saving of Men Armed with Offensive Weapons   None shall save a man who hath his offensive arms in his hands upon pain of losing his prisoner.

7

Flinging Away Powder   Whosoever in skirmish shall fling away his Powder out of his bandileer, that he may sooner come off, shall be punished with death.

8

Embezzelling of the Prey   No soldier shall embezzel any part of the prey, till it be disposed of by the Lord Generall, or others authorized, upon pain of death.

9

Concealing of Prisoners   No officer or soldier shall ransom, or conceal a prisoner, but within twelve hours shall make the same known to the Lord Generall, or others authorized, upon pain of death.

10

Pillaging without Licence   No man upon any good success, shall fall a pillaging before licence, or a sign given, upon pain of death.

11

Retreating before Handy-Blowes   A regiment or company of horse or foot, that chargeth the enemy, and retreat before they come to handy-strokes, shall answer it before a Councell of War; and if the fault be found in the officers, they shall be banished the camp, if in the soldiers, then every tenth man shall be punished at discretion, and the rest serve for Pionees and Scavengers, till a worthy exploit take off that blot.

OF THE DUTIES OF COMMANDERS AND OFFICERS IN PARTICULAR

1

Commanders Must See God Daily Served All commanders are straightly charged to see Almighty God reverently served, and Sermons and Prayers duly frequented.

2

Commanders Must Acquaint my Lord General with Dangerous Humours
All commanders and officers that find any of discontented humour, apt to mutinize or any swerving from direction given, or from the policy of the army set down, shall straightway aquaint the Lord Generall therewith, or others authorized, as they will answer their neglect.

3

Defraud of soldiers' pay Any officer that dare presume to defraud the soldiers of their pay, or any part of it, shall be cashiered.

4

Stopping of Duellers No Corporal, or other officer commanding the Watch, shall willingly suffer a soldier to go forth to a Duel, or private fight, upon pain of death.

5

Drunken and Quarrelsome Officers What officer soever shall come drunk to his guard, or shall quarrel in the quarter, or commit any disorder, shall be cashiered without mercy, and the next officer under him shall have his place, which he may pretend to be his right, and it shall not be refused to him.

6

Careless Captains A captain that is careless in the training and governing of his company, shall be displaced of his charge.

7

Officers Outstaying their Pass   All captains and officers that shall outstay their pass, shall be punished at the Lord Generall's discretion.

8

All Officers to Part Quarrels   All officers of what condition soever shall have power to part quarrels and frays, or sudain disorders betwixt the soldiers, though it be in any other Regiment or Company, and to commit the disordered to prison for the present until such officers as they belong unto are aquainted with it; and what soldier soever shall resist, disobey, or draw his sword against such an officer (although he be no officer of his Regiment or Company) shall be punished with death.

9

Officers non Resident in Garrison   A Captain or officer non resident in the place assigned him for Garrison with Licence, shall have one month's pay defaulted for the first offence, and two months for the second, upon the third offence he shall be discharged of his command.

10

Cashiering of Soldiers   After the army is come to the general Rendevous, no captain shall cashier any soldier that is enrolled, without special warrant of the Lord Generall.

11

Mustering of False and Counterfeit Troops   No captain or officer of a troope or company, shall present in Musters, any but reall Troopers and Soldiers, such as by their pay are bound to follow their Colours, upon pain of cashiering without mercy; and if any Victualler, Freebooter, Enterloper, or soldier whatsoever, of any troop or company shall present himself, or his horse in the Muster, to mislead the Muster-Master, and to betray the Service, the same shall be punished with death.

Commissaries of Victuals and Ammunition Must be True   No Provider, Keeper or officer of Victuall or Ammunition, shall imbezell or spoil any part thereof or give any false account to the Lord Generall, upon pain of death.

THE DUTY OF MUSTER-MASTERS

1

Muster-Masters Conniving at Counterfeits   No Muster-master must wittingly let any pass in the Musters, but such as are really of the Troop or Company presented, upon pain of death.

2

Captains Must Send a Roll of their Men to the Lord General   All captains shall cause their Troops or Companies to be full and complete, and two days after the General Mustering, they shall send to the Lord Generall a perfect list or Roll of all the officers of their troops and companies, and likewise of all the troopers and soldiers that are in actual service, putting down distinctly on the head of each man his Monthly pay.

3

Every Pay-Day   The like roll or list shall the captains send to the Lord Generall, and to the Treasurer of the Army upon every pay-day, during the service with a punctuall expression at the bottom of the said roll, what new troopers or soldiers have been entertained since the last pay-day in lieu of such as are either deceased or cashiered, and likewise the day whereon they were so cashiered and entertained.

4

Subscribed by All the Officers of the Troop or Company   Which said list or roll shall be subscribed, not only by the Captain and his Lieutenant and Coronet or Ensigne, but also by the Sargeants and Corporals respectively, who shall declare upon their Oath that the Troopers and soldiers enrolled in the said list, are reall and actual Troopers or Soldiers of the respective troops and companies, and whosoever shall be convicted of falsehood in any of the Premises, shall be cashiered.

5

Muster-Masters Must Use No Other rolls   No Muster-Master shall presume to receive or accept of any roll to make the Musters by, but the forementioned rolls, upon pain of the loss of his place, and other punishment at discretion.

6

Counterfeit Names in the Rolls   No man shall presume to present himself to the muster, or to be enrolled in the Muster-Rolls by a counterfeit name, or surname, or place of birth, upon pain of death.

OF VICTUALLERS
1
Victuallers Issuing Naughty Victuals   No victuallers shall presume to issue or sell unto any of the Army, unsound, unsavoury, or unwholesome victuals, upon pain of imprisonment, and further Arbitrary punishment.

2
No Soldier Must Be a Victualler   No soldier shall be a victualler without the consent of the Lord Generall, or others authorized upon pain of punishment at discretion.

3
Unseasonable Hours Kept by Victuallers   No victualler shall entertain any soldier in his house or tent, or hut, after the Warningpiece at night, or before they be appraised by the Marshall Generall, upon severe punishment.

OF ADMINISTRATION OF JUSTICE
1
Summary Proceedings   All controversies between soldiers and their captains, and all others, shall be summarily heard and determined by the Councell of War except the weightiness of the cause require further deliberation.

2
The Provost Marshall Must Look to his Prisoner   All officers and others who shall send up any prisoners unto the Marshall Generall of the army, shall likewise deliver unto the Marshall the cause and reason of the imprisonment, and without such cause and reason shown, the Marshall is expressly forbid to take charge of the prisoner. When a prisoner is committed to the charge of the Marshall Generall, the information of the crime, which he standeth committed for, is to be given into the Advocate of the army, within 48 hrs, after the committment, or else for default thereof, the prisoner to be released except good cause be shown wherefore the information cannot be ready within that time.

3
Good of the Destine   The goods of such as dye in the army or garrison, or be slain in the service, if they make any will by word or writing, shall be disposed of according to their Will. If they make no will, then they shall go to their wives or next Kin. If no wife or kindred appear within a year after, shall be disposed of by the appointment of the Lord Generall, according to Laws Civil and Military.

4
Civil Magistrates Imprisoning Soldiers   No magistrate of Town or Country, shall without licence imprison any soldier, unless for Capital Offence.

5
For Debts and Other Small Offences   In matters of debts or trespass, or other inferior cases, the Magistrate shall aquaint his Captain, or other chief officer therewith, who is to end the matter with the consent of the complainant, or to leave the party grieved to take his remedy by due course of Law, And if the officer fail of his duty therein, the Lord Generall upon complaint of the party grieved, will not only see him righted, but the officer punished for his neglect on his behalf.

6
Braving the Court of Justice   No man shall presume to use any braving or menacing words, Signs, or gestures, while the Court of Justice is sitting, upon pain of death.

7
Receiving of Run-Awayes   No inhabitant of City, Town or Country, shall presume to receive any soldier into his service or conceal, or use means to convey such Run-awayes, but shall apprehend all such, and deliver them to the Provost Marshall.

8
Detecting of Offenders   All Captains, officers and soldiers shall doe their endeavors to detect, apprehend and bring to punishment all offenders, and shall assist the officers of the army for that purpose, as they will answer their slackness in the Marshall's Court.

9

If the marshall shall dismisse without authority, any prisoner committed unto his charge, or suffer him to make an escape, he shall be liable to the same punishment due unto the dismissed or escaped offender.

10

Officers Whatsoever to be Punished by the Laws of War   All other faults, disorders, and offences not mentioned in these Articles, shall be punished according to the general customs of war.

And to the end that these lawes and Ordinances be made more public and known, as well to the Officers, as to the common soldiers, every Colonel and Captain is to provide some of these Bookes, and to cause them to be forthwith distinctly and audibly read in every severall Regiment, by the Respective Marshals in presence of all the officers; in the Horse Quarters by sound of trumpet; and amongst the Foot by beat of Drum. And weekly afterwards upon the pay-day every Captain is to cause the same to be read to his owne Company, in presence of his officers. And also upon every main-Guard, the Captain is to do the like, that none may be ignorant of the Lawes and Duties required by them.

Finis

Index